Navigating Life with Purpose & Efficiency

SEAMLESS FLOW

Everyday Productivity

By Jane Sha

Published by Eddy Infomedia
Email: Eddyinfo18@gmail.com
First Edition
First Printing: June 2024
ASIN: B0D2J16357

ISBN: 978-93-341-2952-6

Author's Note: I would like to extend my gratitude to all who supported me throughout the creation of this book. Your encouragement and feedback have been invaluable.

Contact Information:
For feedback, inquiries, or more information, please contact Jane Sha.
Email: janeshainfo@gmail.com

DEDICATION

My sons

CONTENT

Also by Jane Sha

Eddy Pro Planner – Productivity Diary

FOREWARD

This book Seamless Flow by Jane Sha could be truly called a GUIDE towards a purposeful human life.

G - grasping ideas from most notable examples in human history,

U - understanding their interplay to differentiate between true vibration and noise,

I - inspiring towards the right path of self-discovery,

D - developing a self-sustaining & reinforcing process,

E - enlightening on what it means to be human.

The book is an example of seamless flow in itself as it is structured like chain of thoughts one leading to another towards a destination. Jane has seamlessly interwoven materialistic thoughts with spirituality, western mindset with eastern feel, classical deterministic model with quantum probabilistic one, all in one book. This kind of work isn't possible unless it is a life experience. In a way this book gives the reader an insight into author's self-discovery path and process. In this way this work helps others by sharing personal life experience showing the noble intention of the author.

While the book mentions beautifully that journey is more important than the destination, the process is more valuable than the outcome, goal setting is important but only to guide towards a path. Most of the successful people would tell you that their outcomes almost always exceeded their original goals. That's the true test of a journey well-travelled, or a life lived with full potential.

One of the foremost things that is essential to attain our true human potential is to recognise with gratefulness the importance of being human on this planet in the first place. Secondly, understanding that we are an integral part of this design of universe in which we are supposed to manifest universe within us into a reflection around us. Thirdly, we are carrying a lot of information in our genetic code in which lies the secret of living a purposeful and blissful life.

This clear understanding comes from Vedic wisdom which we consider in India as the manuals of this universe. True potential of human life comes our way when we start harnessing our intuition-based capacities as against intellect-based ones, in other words when we use our sixth sense to understand the true nature of reality. Yoga meditation allow us to develop that sixth sense as we control our five senses which are essential for survival but really the distractions if the aim is to achieve true potential of exponential and disproportionate outcomes. This book is being released in June 2024, quite fitting to the occasion of 10th International Day of Yoga which the whole world would celebrate on 21 June 2024.

I conclude by wishing the author Jane Sha all the success in her future endeavours like this one which surely create value to the readers with life changing potential.

- ***H.E. Raj Kumar Srivastava,***

Indian Ambassador to Croatia

PREFACE

Innovation and Creativity have become the cornerstones of progress and productivity. Disruption across all walks of life is at a scale that has been unimagined. The world is fast changing, and all we need is some anchors for us to navigate life with purpose and efficiency.

I was pleasantly surprised to see the author, Jane Sha, put together a super exciting book, Seamless Flow. It is a masterful guide that offers a profound and transformative journey into the realm of maximizing your productivity. This book isn't just a manual for maximizing your productivity; it's a blueprint for crafting a life filled with success, fulfilment and boundless possibilities.

In a world inundated with the noise of the mundane, Seamless Flow stands out as a lighthouse, guiding you towards your true potential. The principles, practical strategies and actionable steps within these pages are not just theories but the author's own time tested, actionable insights that can help you engineer your imagination for remarkable success in all areas of life. From business ventures to personal relationships, this book has the power to transform how you approach challenges and opportunities.

This book is on a very relevant topic which will inspire and ignite readers. All the topics and examples quoted in such a lucid form with so much simplicity is remarkable.

I found the book eminently interesting, relevant and stimulating. I am sure and confident that every reader will emerge with something to think about and a lot to apply.

I invite you to embark on this exhilarating journey through the corridors of purpose and efficiency. With this book, you will learn to paint your own canvas of productivity, one vibrant stroke at a time. Whether you are an entrepreneur seeking innovation, an artist searching for inspiration or an individual striving for personal growth, this book offers the tools to engineer your imagination and sculpt your destiny.

With great enthusiasm, I encourage you to embrace the profound wisdom within these pages and embark on a productive journey.

A profound book that talks about the mindset, toolset and skillset in a seamless flow to navigate your life with purpose and efficiency. Once you start to apply and practice these principles and steps you will get wings to think big and fly high!

- **Shyam Iyer**
- **Founder & CEO**
- **60 Bits Consulting**

INTRODUCTION

Time plays a dual role in the symphony of life, serving as both conductor and composer. It orchestrates the moments that shape our journey and composes the melody of our existence. Despite the perpetual pace of passing hours, we often fail to appreciate the fleeting beauty of each moment and the opportunities that come with it.

How often do we pause to truly appreciate each moment? How often do we seize the opportunities that bloom before us, recognising them as the fair flowers of our potential?

Welcome to this journey, that goes beyond the mere passage of time and delves deep into the art of mastering productivity. It uncovers the secrets to harnessing its power and transforming it into the fuel for achieving our goals.

Productivity is not merely about doing more in less time, but about making conscious choices that align with our goals and aspirations. It is about cultivating a mindset of purposeful action, where every moment is infused with meaning and every endeavour is a step towards realising our highest potential.

In a world where distractions and demands pull us in countless directions, it's easy to lose sight of the profound significance of each passing moment. Yet, within the available time lies the potential for transformation, growth, and the realisation of our deepest aspirations.

Like fair flowers blooming in their prime, our opportunities for growth and fulfilment are fleeting. It is incumbent upon us, therefore, to cultivate a mindset of purposeful action, to make every moment count, and to seize the advantages that time presents.

Seamless Flow is an everyday productivity guide designed to help you navigate through the clutter of daily tasks and distractions towards a more productive and fulfilling life.

Productivity is not just about doing more; it's about doing what matters most, and doing it well.

This book is for anyone who has ever felt overwhelmed by

1. To-do list.
2. Struggled to maintain focus in an age of constant interruptions.
3. Simply wished there were more hours in the day.
4. In search of finding purpose in life.

If you are someone looking to make the most out of your personal time; the insights within these pages can help.

We'll explore what productivity truly means, demystify common misconceptions, and provide practical insights that you can apply to your daily routine.

- **Jane Sha**

Author, Consultant & Public Speaker

PART 1 UNDERSTANDING PRODUCTIVITY

1 MISCONCEPTIONS

Make use of time, let not advantage slip;
Beauty within itself should not be wasted:
Fair flowers that are not gather'd in their prime Rot and consume themselves in little time.

- William Shakespeare

Productivity is a concept often misunderstood and oversimplified in the modern world. It's easy to fall into the trap of equating productivity with sheer quantity of tasks completed, emails answered, or hours logged. Productivity transcends beyond the mere act of busyness; it's about the deliberate allocation of our most valuable resource which is time.

True productivity is not squeezing more into your day but about prioritising what truly matters. It's about aligning your actions with your goals, zeroing in on the tasks that propel you forward, and ensuring every step you take gets you closer to your dreams.

Imagine a sculptor chiselling away at a block of marble. Each strike of the hammer is deliberate, and purposeful, aimed at revealing the beauty hidden within the rough stone. In much the same way, true productivity involves the careful selection of tasks, the mindful allocation of resources, and the relentless pursuit of excellence in all that we do.

In this fast-paced world, it's all too easy to become overwhelmed by the constant stream of demands vying for our attention. We find ourselves pulled in countless directions, juggling competing priorities and struggling to maintain a sense of balance amidst the chaos.

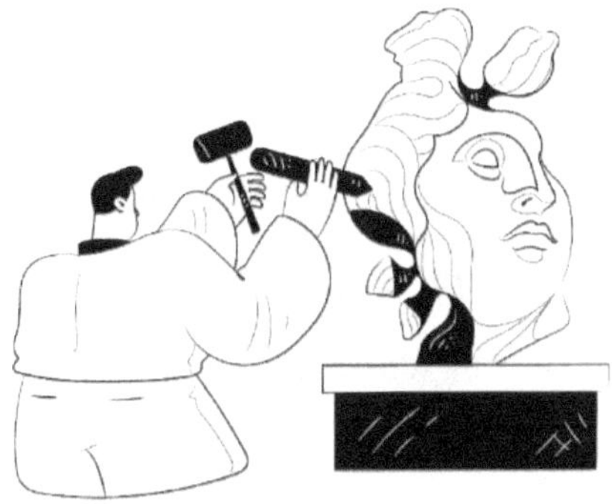

Carving the Way for Result

Amidst the noise and confusion, *it's essential to remember the fundamental principles of productivity - clarity of purpose, focus of effort and alignment with our deepest values.*

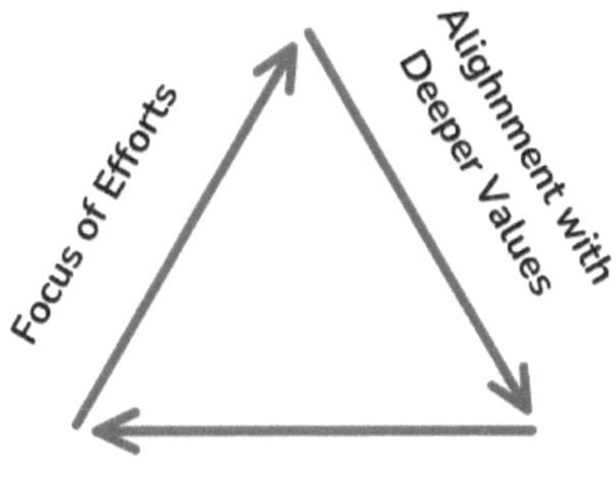

Fundamental Principle of Productivity

Productivity, then, is not just about ticking items off a to-do list or working longer hours; it's about being thoughtful and not a handful. It's about leveraging our time and energy in the most efficient and effective manner possible, maximising our output while minimising unnecessary effort and attention.

Achieving true productivity requires more than just time management techniques or productivity hacks; it requires a fundamental shift in mindset. It requires us to let go of the illusion of busyness and embrace the discipline of purposeful action. It requires us to be intentional in our choices, to prioritise ruthlessly, and to stay true to our vision, even in the face of adversity.

Productivity is not measured by the number of tasks completed or hours worked but by the impact we have on the world around us. It's about making a meaningful contribution, leaving a legacy that transcends the confines of time itself. In that sense, productivity becomes not just a means to an end but a philosophy of life - a way of living and working that honours our deepest aspirations and celebrates the boundless potential of the human spirit.

Our brains are like a wild jungle gym of thoughts and feelings, playing tricks on our focus. The pursuit of productivity has become more critical than ever. Yet, productivity remains an elusive goal, often hindered by the complex interplay of psychological factors that influence our behaviour.

The struggle is real!

By delving deeper into the intricacies of human cognition and motivation, we can uncover valuable insights that not only shed light on our productivity challenges but also provide a roadmap for developing more effective work habits. Let's delve into some common productivity myths and explore better ways to achieve what matters.

Misconception 1: Being Busy

In our quest to accomplish more tasks, we've forgotten the real essence of productivity. One of the most pervasive myths in today's fast-paced world is that being constantly busy is synonymous with being productive. Being busy is often seen as a virtue, rewarded for its association with hard work. This misconception leads many to pack their schedules with tasks, meetings, and commitments, often measuring their worth by how full their calendar appears. However, being busy does not necessarily mean making meaningful progress toward goals. True productivity isn't about filling every moment with activity; *it's about strategically choosing what to focus on and ensuring those tasks align with objectives.*

The relentless pursuit of productivity, fuelled by endless tips, tricks, and tools, can paradoxically result in procrastination, stress, burnout, and disillusionment. Moreover, it has stripped away our capacity to simply enjoy our own company. The cult of extreme productivity has convinced us that boredom is something to be feared and that idleness is only for the lazy.

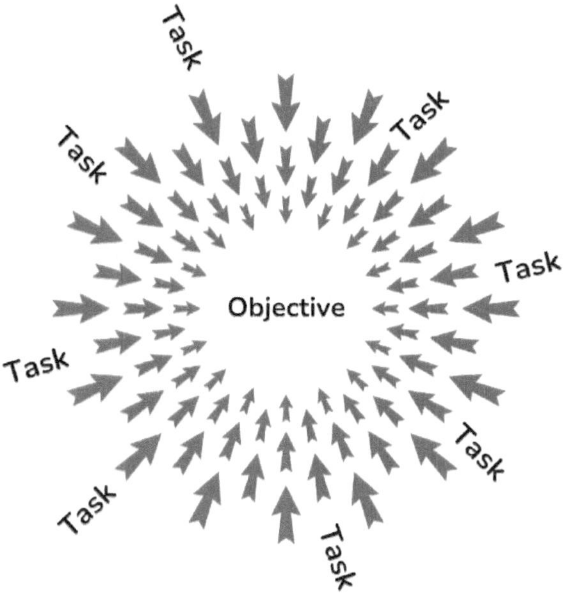

Objective Based Tasks

Albert Einstein, one of history's most brilliant minds, defied the modern obsession with constant busyness. While his annus mirabilis of 1905 saw him revolutionise physics with groundbreaking papers on relativity, mass-energy equivalence, and the photoelectric effect, Einstein's approach to productivity stood in stark contrast to today's relentless "hustle culture."

In the contemporary workplace, the belief pervades that a packed schedule and long office hours signify true dedication and productivity. This mindset mistakenly equates busyness with effectiveness, often leading to burnout and a lack of fulfilment. Einstein, however, understood the vital importance of solitude, reflection, and activities that rejuvenated his mind and spirit. Be it playing music, sailing, or spending time in nature, he prioritised moments of leisure that allowed him to recharge.

For Einstein, uninterrupted periods of deep thought were integral, not distractions. Solitude provided the mental space to wander, ponder complex problems, and arrive at intuitive leaps - insights that may have eluded him in a perpetually harried environment. Yet he also embraced the value of engaging dialogue. Einstein maintained a close circle where he could freely discuss theories and quandaries, often during casual walks. This collaborative approach underscored that productivity transcends solitary work; it is profoundly enriched by sharing perspectives with others.

Einstein's most fruitful eras struck a harmonious balance between profound individual focus and lively peer interactions, anchored by a lifestyle that prioritised leisure and curiosity over sheer busyness. This paradigm redefined productivity as a creative pursuit valuing quality over quantity of work.

Cultivating such creatively productive approaches demands a deliberate shift in our modern mindset and practices. We must prioritise "deep work" by dedicating uninterrupted time for immersion in complex, meaningful tasks, with stretches of profound contemplation. We must recognise how breaks and leisure activities stimulate creativity and problem-solving prowess. And we must foster opportunities for enriching conversations and collaborations that enhance understanding and catalyse fresh ideas. Maintaining a healthy work-life balance that fulfils both professional and personal spheres is vital for holistic well-being.

True effectiveness lies not in cramming each moment with work, but in focusing energy on what genuinely matters - embracing curiosity, making space for leisure and collaborative engagement. By redefining productivity through the lens of impact and fulfilment rather than mere busyness, we unlock our highest potential to contribute with passion and purpose.

Misconception 2: Multitasking

Human brain is optimised for focused,

not divided attention.

Another widespread belief is the effectiveness of multitasking. Many pride themselves on their ability to juggle multiple tasks at once, believing it to be a hallmark of efficiency. However, research consistently shows that multitasking can be detrimental to productivity. Multitasking can reduce productivity significantly specially for intricate tasks. The human brain is not wired to focus on multiple tasks with high efficiency.

The human brain is finely tuned for focused attention rather than divided attention. Our cognitive architecture is optimised to concentrate on specific tasks or stimuli, allowing us to delve deeply into complex problems, engage in creative endeavours, and absorb information with clarity and depth.

When we focus our attention on a single task or idea, our brain allocates its resources more efficiently, enabling us to process information more effectively and make connections that might otherwise go unnoticed. This focused attention allows us to enter a state of flow, where time seems to melt away, and we become fully immersed in the task at hand.

Juggling Tasks Doesn't Equal Productivity

In contrast, divided attention attempting to multitask or juggle multiple stimuli simultaneously can overload our cognitive systems and diminish our ability to perform tasks optimally. While we may feel like we're being more productive by multitasking, research suggests that our brains are not designed to handle such cognitive overload efficiently. Instead of enhancing productivity, dividing our attention can lead to decreased performance, increased stress levels, and reduced overall effectiveness.

What we perceive as multitasking is often just rapid task-switching, which can lead to increased errors, reduced quality of work, and a greater cognitive load, ultimately slowing us down.

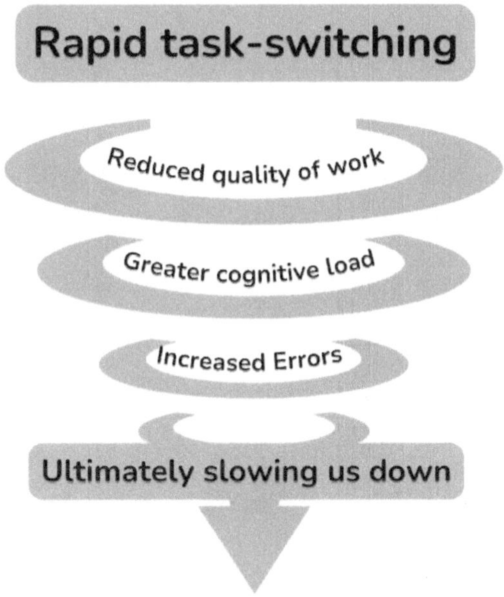

Cost of Rapid task switching

Our brains may seem adept at juggling multiple tasks simultaneously, but in reality, what's happening is a constant shifting of attention from one task to another. This continuous switching between tasks can come at a cost, leading to a range of negative consequences that ultimately impede our productivity and effectiveness.

The belief in its effectiveness stems from the desire to accomplish more within limited time frames. Our brains switch focus from one task to another, but not without cost. Each switch incurs what's known as a switching cost in terms of time and mental bandwidth, leading to decreased efficiency and increased likelihood of errors. This is because multitasking divides the brain's resources, which can dilute focus and weaken performance on each task. Over time, this can also lead to mental fatigue, further diminishing productivity and the quality of work produced.

The Costs of Context Switching: Why Multitasking Slows You Down

Cognitive psychology encompasses several types of "expenses" incurred when transitioning from one task to another. These costs can significantly impact productivity, efficiency, and the quality of the work being performed. Whenever you switch tasks, there's a ramp-up period needed to familiarise yourself with where you left off and what needs to be done next. This can be especially pronounced if the tasks are complex or require different sets of skills or knowledge bases. After an interruption, it takes time to recover your train of thought and return to a pre-interruption level of performance. Research suggests it can take over 20 minutes to fully regain focus after an interruption.

Juggling multiple tasks, especially complex ones, can drain cognitive resources faster than focusing on a single task, leading to mental fatigue. This can reduce our overall cognitive capacity for tasks later in the day. With divided attention, the likelihood of making mistakes increases. Each task switch might introduce a small error, but these can accumulate, leading to a significant impact on the overall quality of work. Task-switching can impair short-term memory, making it harder to keep track of multiple threads or pieces of information. This can lead to confusion or the need to redo work to correct forgotten details. Constantly switching tasks and feeling like you're not making progress on any of them can lead to increased stress and anxiety. This emotional toll can further detract from work quality and personal well-being.

The inability to immerse deeply in a task can reduce the satisfaction and engagement derived from work, potentially impacting motivation and long-term job satisfaction. *Deep work is a prolonged period of focused concentration on a cognitively demanding task. It's a state where distractions are minimised, and the mind is fully absorbed in the challenge at hand.*

When Deep Focus Leads to Breakthroughs

Engaging deeply in a single task, often referred to as entering a state of flow, allows for more significant insights and breakthroughs. Frequent switching prevents reaching this depth, potentially leading to missed opportunities for innovation or higher-quality outcomes. Focused, uninterrupted work is conducive to learning and skill mastery. Constantly switching tasks can hinder the ability to develop expertise in a particular area, as deep and deliberate practice is often necessary for such advancements.

In the heart of the 17th century, as the Great Plague of London wrought havoc across the city, a young Isaac Newton found himself compelled to leave the intellectual hub of Cambridge behind. With the University of Cambridge temporarily closed to stem the spread of the disease, Newton retreated to the tranquil confines of his family estate in Wools Thorpe. Little did he know, this forced isolation would mark the beginning of one of the most extraordinary periods of scientific discovery in history, later dubbed his "annus mirabilis" or "year of wonders."

In this period of unparalleled concentration, Newton embarked on a series of explorations that would forever alter the course of science. With nothing but time and his thoughts, he began to unravel the mysteries of calculus, a new mathematical language that would provide the tools for generations of scientists to decode the universe's secrets. His inquiries into the nature of light led to groundbreaking advances in optics, challenging long-held beliefs and opening new vistas in the understanding of vision and colour.

But perhaps his most monumental achievements were yet to come. In the quiet of Wools Thorpe, amidst the apple orchards that whispered the secrets of the universe, Newton formulated his laws of motion. These principles laid the very foundations of classical mechanics, offering a framework to understand the movement of objects from the smallest particles to celestial bodies. With the same focused attention, he conceived the universal law of gravitation, a theory so profound that revealed the force that keeps the planets in their orbits and the apple falling to the ground.

Newton's year at Wools Thorpe stands as a testament to the incredible feats the human mind can achieve when granted the luxury of undivided attention. By dedicating himself entirely to the pursuit of knowledge, free from the interruptions of the external world, he was able to forge insights that would illuminate the path of science for centuries to come.

The allure of multitasking lies in the illusion of progress; by engaging in multiple activities, we feel productive. However, this scattered focus often leads to half-completed tasks and a diminished ability to perform complex problem-solving or creative thinking. The key to productivity lies in focused effort and prioritisation; choosing a single task to dedicate one's attention to and seeing it through to completion before moving on to the next task.

Not all tasks hold equal value, and understanding which tasks are most impactful can help in allocating time and resources more effectively. Prioritisation ensures that our efforts are concentrated on tasks that truly move the needle.

While the myths of constant busyness and multitasking are deeply ingrained in our cultural understanding of work and productivity, they are fundamentally flawed. True productivity arises from intentional, focused effort on tasks that align with one's goals and priorities.

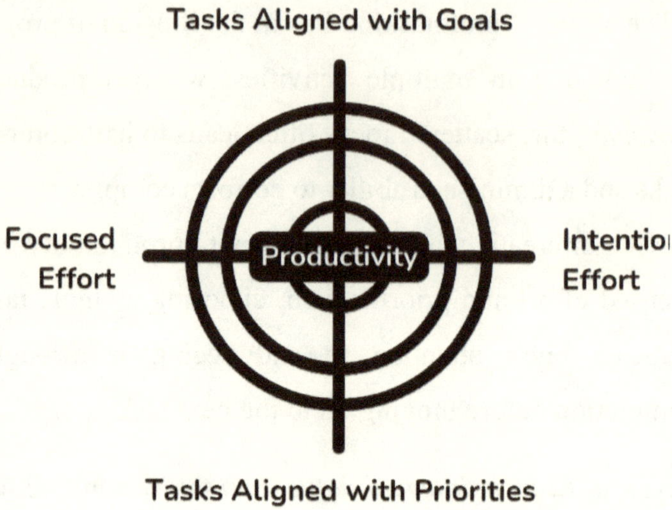
Tasks Aligned with Goals
Focused
Effort
Productivity
Intentio
Effort
Tasks Aligned with Priorities

Misconception 3: Being organised

Being organised is considered synonymous with being productive. Many people equate productivity with having meticulously planned schedules, color-coded calendars, and neatly organised to-do lists. Being organised helps in managing tasks and time efficiently. It helps in prioritising schedule. It seems contradictory that using productive tools is not the same as being productive. However, the problem lies in becoming overly fixated on organising rather than the substance of productivity.

Striving to be perfectly organised can lead us to a state of paralysis, where we become so fixated on arranging and categorising tasks, that we struggle to take meaningful action. In the pursuit of perfection in our organising systems, we inadvertently suppress creativity and spontaneity, ultimately hindering our productivity rather than enhancing it. We sideline the ultimate goal and get busy in the everlasting process.

An overzealous focus on structure can stifle creativity. The spark of inspiration often emerges from unexpected moments, and rigid schedules can leave no room for happy accidents. Over-organising can also lead to a fear of making mistakes, hindering the exploration that's essential for innovation. A structure keeps us focused, but a touch of spontaneity allows for the unexpected bursts of brilliance.

Creativity thrives on a little chaos. While organisation keeps us on track, an overreliance on structure can squeeze the life out of our ideas. Imagine a painter meticulously planning every stroke, their masterpiece might lack the vibrancy that comes from spontaneous expression. The same goes for problem-solving, sometimes the solution arrives during a casual walk, not a rigidly planned brainstorming session. Over-organising can also breed a fear of mistakes, hindering the exploration that's vital for innovation. Leaving room for spontaneity allows for those unexpected bursts of brilliance that can truly transform our work.

Imagine yourself striving for inbox zero every day. You dedicate significant time and effort to checking and organising your emails, aiming to end each day with an empty inbox. You create elaborate filing systems, meticulously categorising and sorting emails into folders to maintain this elusive goal.

Chaos to Creativity

However, despite your best efforts, you may find that this relentless pursuit of organising doesn't necessarily align with your larger priorities. While you may achieve the satisfaction of an empty inbox, you may also realise that it hasn't translated into significant progress on your important work or strategic objectives.

A study from IBM researchers, suggests that the time spent organising emails into folders may not result in faster retrieval compared to simply searching for them.

The pursuit of organising everything becomes a time-consuming endeavour that doesn't align with broader goals or enhance productivity. Instead of obsessing over emptying the inbox, benefit more from focusing on tasks that contribute directly to professional objectives and overall well-being.

View organising as a means to an end rather than an end in itself. Use organisational tools and systems to support your productivity goals, but don't let them overshadow the importance of actually getting things done. Do not make organising goals as productivity goals. Organising is only one part of productivity and not the ultimate goal.

Being over-focused on organising, takes away the fun and creative part of life. Imagine your friend meticulously planning a day trip to a new destination. Every aspect of the outing is carefully organised, leaving no room for error. As you embark on the adventure, your friend is consumed with running the schedule, managing every minute detail, and darting from one place to another.

In the pursuit of sticking to the plan, you begin to notice that the enjoyment of the present moment is slipping away. Your friend's mind is so occupied with the logistics of the day that there's little space left to simply be present and appreciate the experience. Instead of savouring the sights and sounds of the new destination, you find yourselves caught up in the process, rushing from one attraction to the next.

Despite the excitement of exploring a new place, you can't help but feel that something is missing. The spontaneity and creativity that make adventures truly memorable seem to be overshadowed by the rigid adherence to the plan. While the day may unfold smoothly according to schedule, the joy of discovery is diminished by the overwhelming focus on organising.

In the end, you realise that while meticulous planning has its merits, it's equally important to leave room for spontaneity and enjoyment of the present moment. Life's adventures are meant to be savoured, not simply checked off a list.

Misconception 4: Making the most of your day

The notion that using each moment of the day to achieve success, overlooks the importance of rest, reflection, and renewal in maintaining long-term productivity and well-being. While it's tempting to fill every moment of the day with tasks and activities, the reality is that humans are not machines. We need time to recharge and rejuvenate in order to perform at our best. Constantly pushing ourselves to the limit without allowing for breaks can lead to burnout, decreased motivation, and diminished creativity.

Productivity is not the same as efficient time management, rather productivity is the defined goal management.

Without proper breaks, adequate rest and relaxation, we experience increased stress levels, fatigue, and decreased overall satisfaction with life. When we are constantly occupied with tasks and activities, we do not have the mental space to think creatively or come up with innovative ideas. Embracing moments of boredom and allowing the mind to wander can lead to breakthrough insights and new perspectives.

Overloading the day with tasks and activities can actually decrease focus and productivity in the long run. Without breaks to recharge and reset, we will experience mental fatigue and decreased cognitive function, making it harder to concentrate and complete tasks efficiently. Rather than striving to make use of every single moment of the day, it's important to find a balance between activity and rest.

Instead of trying to do everything at once, prioritise goal-based tasks and activities. Focus on completing high-priority tasks during peak energy times and allow for breaks in between to rest and recharge.

Whether it's taking a short walk, practicing mindfulness, or simply sitting quietly, make time for activities that promote well-being and renewal. Instead of filling every moment of the day with stimulation and activity, embrace moments of boredom and allow your mind to wander. Boredom can be a catalyst for creativity and innovation, leading to new ideas and insights.

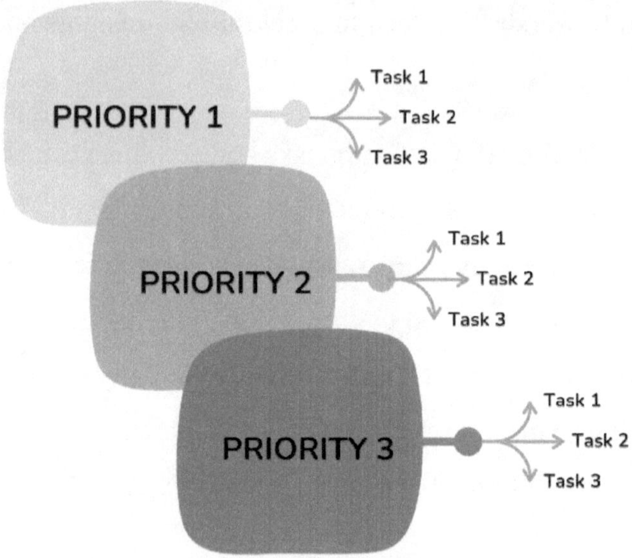

Prioritise Tasks

Just the way you schedule important meetings and appointments, schedule downtime for rest and relaxation.

Be gentle with yourself and recognise that it's okay to have moments of rest, relaxation, and downtime. Embrace imperfection and allow yourself the flexibility to adapt and adjust your schedule as needed.

Misconception 5: Set audacious goals

An audacious goal and having a big vision are distinct concepts, though they are often intertwined in discussions about productivity and success. Having a big vision involves conceptualising a broader, more expansive picture of the future. It encompasses your aspirations, values, and overarching purpose in life or in a particular endeavour. Takes you toward a larger purpose or goal. For instance, envisioning a world where clean energy powers communities or imagining a society where education is accessible to all are examples of big visions.

Goals timeline

Whereas, Goals are milestones that guide us to reach a desired destination. While it's important to have ambitious goals, simply thinking big can be counterproductive. Success is not solely determined by the scale of one's goals. Simply thinking big without a clear plan or actionable steps can be counterproductive. Merely envisioning grandiose outcomes without considering the practicalities and challenges involved can result in wasted time, resources, and effort.

For example, committing to run a half marathon when you're just starting out with running or aiming to publish a novel without prior experience in writing can be overwhelming and daunting. In the long run, this can lead to viewing the activity—whether it's running or writing—as intimidating and overwhelming. The pressure to achieve such lofty goals within a short timeframe can result in burnout and disillusionment, causing you to associate the activity with stress and failure.

It's important to set realistic and achieve near-term goals that align with your current abilities and interests, keeping in mind the larger picture of life and vision. For that break down larger goals into smaller, manageable steps, allowing yourself to progress gradually and build confidence along the way. Celebrate small victories and be patient with yourself as you work toward your goals.

Someone who has a big vision of running a full marathon of 26.2 miles, but hasn't even started training yet. Simply fixating on the grandiose goal of completing a marathon without a clear plan or actionable steps can be overwhelming and counterproductive. Break down the goal into smaller, achievable steps can pave the way to success. Instead of immediately committing to running a full marathon, begin by setting smaller, more attainable goals such as running a few kilometres a few times a week. Start with a manageable distance that feels comfortable and gradually increase the distance as you build endurance and confidence.

Break down the training schedule into weekly or monthly increments, gradually increasing the distance and intensity of your runs over time. Break down the journey to running a marathon into smaller milestone goals, such as completing a 5K race, then a 10K race, followed by a half marathon 21 kilometres. Each milestone achieved builds confidence and momentum, propelling you closer to your ultimate goal. Consider seeking guidance from experienced runners or hiring a coach who can provide personalised training advice and support. Joining a running group or community can also provide motivation, accountability, and camaraderie along the way. Each small goal achieved builds momentum and confidence, ultimately leading you closer to realising your big vision of crossing the finish line of a full marathon.

Starting with a big vision is admirable, but attempting to tackle a huge goal right off the bat can often lead to breakdowns and frustration. To create a breakthrough and achieve sustainable progress, it's essential to break down vision into smaller, more manageable near-future goals. This approach allows to measure progress, stay motivated, and gradually work towards achieving larger aspirations.

2 OVERCOMING OBSTACLES

Embarking on a journey to enhance productivity is a worthy pursuit with substantial improvements in efficiency and success. Nonetheless, this endeavour is not without obstacles. Here are five common challenges in our quest for heightened productivity.

Obstacle 1: Distractions

Distraction, the diversion of attention away from tasks or goals, poses one of the most persistent challenges to productivity. In today's hyper-connected world, these distractions can come in various forms, such as social media notifications, emails, or interruptions from colleagues. To navigate this obstacle, we must first understand the nature of distractions. They are not merely nuisances but potent forces that chip away at our focus and productivity. Recognising this is the first step in managing distractions and regaining our attention.

Distracted Mind

Distraction pulls our attention in multiple directions and hinder our ability to focus on important tasks. Distractions increase cognitive load, or the amount of mental effort required to complete a task. When our attention is divided between multiple stimuli, our cognitive resources become depleted, leading to decreased performance and accuracy.

Even a brief interruption can significantly impair performance on complex cognitive tasks.

Constantly switching between tasks in response to distractions leads to task-switching costs. Each task switch incurs a cognitive penalty, as our brains need time to refocus and reorient attention. Task-switching can reduce productivity significantly. Effective distraction management relies on attentional control, or the ability to regulate and allocate attention to relevant information while ignoring distractions.

Distractions also contribute to increased stress levels. The constant barrage of notifications, emails, and interruptions can heighten feelings of anxiety and overwhelm, further compromising our ability to concentrate and perform effectively.

The Neuroscience of Distraction

Distractions, whether they stem from external stimuli like noise or internal sources like wandering thoughts, set off a complex chain of events within our brains. They trigger a cascade of neurological responses in our brains, disrupting our attention and impeding cognitive performance.

The prefrontal cortex is responsible for executive functions. It acts as the brain's control center, managing functions such as decision-making, problem-solving, and working memory. When distractions arise, they flood this area with competing signals, overwhelming its capacity to maintain focus and attention which is compromising our ability to stay focused on the task at hand. However, when bombarded with distractions, its resources become stretched thin, impairing its ability to effectively regulate attention.

One key mechanism at play during cognitive overload is the brain's attentional network, which consists of various regions responsible for directing and sustaining attention. Distractions hijack this network, diverting resources away from the task at hand and scattering focus across multiple stimuli.

The brain's limbic system is involved in processing emotions and motivation, also plays a role in the response to distractions. Emotional responses triggered by distractions can further exacerbate cognitive overload, as heightened arousal levels interfere with cognitive processes.

Distractions can trigger the release of stress hormones such as cortisol, which can further impair cognitive function. Chronic exposure to distractions and the resulting stress can lead to cognitive fatigue, diminishing overall productivity and performance over time.

Individual differences in attentional control and susceptibility to distractions influence how we respond to cognitive overload. Factors such as personality traits, stress levels, and environmental factors all play a role in shaping how distractions impact cognitive performance.

Distractions trigger a cascade of neurological responses that disrupt the delicate balance of attention and cognitive processes in the brain. Understanding these mechanisms will help us mitigate the impact of distractions and optimise cognitive performance in various tasks and environments.

Can we overcome distractions?

Learning to overcome distractions is a continuous process. Once we understand why and how are we distracted we can be mindful about minimising them and move towards focused life.

One of the ways of managing distractions is having good attentional control, which allows us to regulate our attention and ignore irrelevant distractions. Those with strong attentional control show greater resistance to distractions and perform better on tasks. They are able to resist distracting stimuli and maintain focus on their tasks Practicing mindfulness will enhance attentional control by training the brain to focus on the present moment and resist distractions.

Individuals with higher levels of attentional control demonstrate better task performance and are less susceptible to the detrimental effects of distractions because they are.

For distraction free state, start by creating a serene, clutter-free workspace. It lays the foundation for minimising external distractions and fostering focused work. Implement digital detoxes such as limiting device access and scheduling technology-free periods will effectively curb the temptation of online distractions.

The incessant ping of notifications for emails, texts, social media updates is a major obstacle to productivity, diverting attention from tasks. Establish specific times for checking emails and social media to resist distractions during focused work periods. Disable notifications on devices during focused work sessions will remove visual cues, allowing undivided attention and guilt-free indulgence during designated breaks. Group similar distracting activities will streamline workflow, minimising the disruptive effects of context switching.

Upon completing a focused work session, reward yourself with designated "distraction time." This positive reinforcement system incentivises sustained focus and provides well-deserved breaks, bolstering motivation for subsequent work periods.

Physical environment has a multiplier impact on our productivity. Create an environment where you can minimise auditory distractions. Our auditory environment poses a significant distraction risk. Constant background noise, from traffic sounds to chatter, can severely impede concentration. Solutions are simple like using noise-cancelling headphones or consider a workspace layout in a quiet corner away from high-traffic areas or talkative colleagues. Even a simple change in location can yield substantial benefits.

Beyond the physical environment, people around us can also disrupt our focus. Communicate your need for uninterrupted work time to colleagues or family members, politely requesting minimal interruptions. Schedule specific meeting times for longer discussions or collaborations, reducing impromptu disruptions. Utilise visual cues like "Do Not Disturb" signs to signal focused work periods, fostering a conducive environment for concentration, even in shared spaces.

By being mindful about internal and external distractions, and taking required steps to manage them, we can create an environment conducive to deep focus, minimising distractions, and maximising productivity.

Obstacle 2: Procrastination

Procrastination is the thief of time.

-Edward Young

The word procrastination originates from the Latin roots "pro," meaning forward, and "crastinatus," meaning till the next day. Procrastination, or the act of delaying tasks despite knowing they need to be done, is often referred to as the thief of time, as it leads to the squandering of valuable resources. Procrastination makes it hard and taxing to finish certain tasks on time, so why do we do this to ourselves?

Procrastination, the act of delaying tasks or activities despite knowing that they need to be done, is a pervasive obstacle to productivity that affects us across various domains of life. It involves delaying tasks or activities, often due to feelings of boredom, anxiety, or a lack of motivation. While procrastination may seem like a mere issue of self-discipline or time management, its roots run deeper into the intricacies of human cognition and behaviour. By examining procrastination through the lens of neuroscience, we can gain insights into why it occurs and how it impacts our productivity.

The Battle Within: Limbic System vs. Prefrontal Cortex

Science reveals that procrastination emerges from a complex interplay between two key regions of the brain: the limbic system and the prefrontal cortex.

At the core of procrastination lies a battle between the limbic system, responsible for instinctual responses and pleasure-seeking behaviours, and the prefrontal cortex, which governs higher-order cognitive functions such as planning and decision-making. When faced with an unpleasant task, the limbic system often dominates, leading to the postponement of tasks and seeking immediate gratification.

The limbic system, often referred to as the "paleomammalian brain," is evolutionarily ancient and dominates many automatic processes in the brain. It triggers instinctual responses, such as the urge to flee from unpleasant situations. Despite its antiquity, the limbic system maintains strong connections with the prefrontal cortex, influencing decision-making processes.

In contrast to the limbic system, the prefrontal cortex is a relatively newer and less developed part of the brain. It is responsible for planning complex behaviours, expressing personality traits, and making decisions. However, due to its comparative weakness, the prefrontal cortex often succumbs to the overpowering influence of the limbic system, leading to procrastination.

The Conflict Between Present and Future Selves

Procrastination can also be viewed as a conflict between the present self, seeking immediate rewards and gratification, and the future self, concerned with long-term goals and outcomes. The present self often prioritises short-term pleasure over long-term benefits, resulting in the delay of essential tasks.

Often, tasks we avoid seem daunting because of our focus on the immediate discomfort they might create.

Procrastination thrives on our tendency to view unpleasant tasks through a distorted lens. We often magnify the difficulty and dread the discomfort they might cause. This negative perception creates a mental barrier that prevents us from even starting.

Despite common beliefs, the notion that individuals perform better under pressure due to procrastination is often an illusion. While procrastination may create a sense of urgency, it can lead to increased stress, decreased productivity, and compromised emotional well-being in the long run.

How is it possible that, knowing what is best, one would choose to act otherwise?

-Socrates

At the core of Socrates' inquiry lies a paradox: the disconnect between knowledge and action. Despite possessing the intellect to discern what is virtuous or beneficial, individuals often find themselves faltering when it comes to translating this knowledge into action.

Procrastination is not merely a time-management issue; it's a complex psychological behaviour that involves delaying tasks perceived as unpleasant, challenging, or overwhelming. This avoidance can stem from various factors, including fear of failure, perfectionism, or a lack of intrinsic motivation. When faced with such tasks, our brain tends to prioritise immediate comfort over long-term benefits, leading us to put off the task in favour of more enjoyable or less daunting activities.

To overcome procrastination and enhance productivity, it is essential to understand the psychological dynamics that underlie our behaviour.

Understanding the intricate workings of the mind will shed light on the persistent habit of procrastination, but unravelling this tendency requires more than just insight, it demands action. One powerful method for overcoming procrastination is the practice of mindfulness. While this term may evoke images of meditation retreats and serene landscapes, mindfulness is, in fact, a simple and accessible practice that anyone can incorporate into their daily lives.

Mindfulness involves cultivating awareness of the present moment, both internally and externally. It's about tuning into the sensations, thoughts, and emotions that arise in response to various triggers or situations. By bringing our attention to the here and now, we can break free from the grip of procrastination and make conscious choices about how we respond to challenges. Mindfulness enables us to observe our habits without judgement, allowing us to recognise the negative impact of procrastination on our well-being.

Central to the practice of mindfulness is the attitude of curiosity. Instead of reacting to discomfort with avoidance or resistance, we can approach it with openness and interest. By exploring our reactions, emotions, and physical sensations with curiosity, we can uncover new insights and perspectives that help break the cycle of procrastination. Mindfulness offers a compelling alternative to procrastination by tapping into the attitudinal quality of curiosity.

Rather than seeking relief through avoidance, we can engage with tasks and challenges with a sense of curiosity and openness. This shift in mindset transforms the experience of work from one of drudgery to one of exploration and discovery. By practising mindfulness, we can gradually rewire our brains to associate productivity with a sense of satisfaction and fulfilment. When we approach tasks with curiosity and engagement, we not only increase our likelihood of completing them but also derive greater enjoyment from the process. This positive experience serves as reinforcement, solidifying our dedication to productive habits while reducing the temptation to procrastinate or stray into aimless exploration.

The Influence-Zone

When our surrounding becomes a battleground of distractions, interruptions, ambiguity, and a lack of structure, it creates a stressful and unproductive environment. Procrastination, in this context, becomes a coping mechanism. By putting off the task, we can temporarily escape the discomfort and overwhelm of the experience zone.

Our behaviour is a complex dance between who we are and the world around us i.e. the environment. It's not just about our internal desires and motivations, but also the situations we find ourselves in, the people we interact with, and even the physical space we occupy. We constantly pick up on subtle cues from others, a smile, a frown, a disapproving glance. These cues can significantly influence our behaviour, even if we're not consciously aware of it. The environment a person is in plays a huge role too. It's like a constant back-and-forth between the person and their surroundings that shapes how they act.

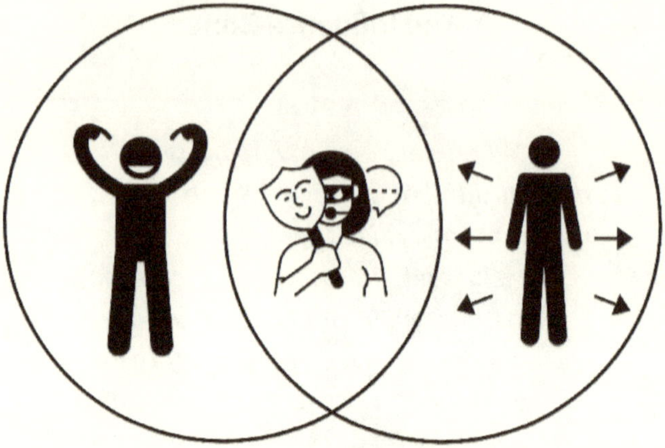

Behaviour Influencers

Behaviour is not solely determined by internal factors such as personality traits or motivations but also shaped by the dynamic interplay between the individual and their surroundings.

Imagine yourself in a swirling mix of everything that surrounds you. It's not just the sights and sounds, but the feelings, expectations, and even the furniture in the room. Let us call it the influence-zone. This zone isn't just about you, but the constant interplay between you and your environment.

This zone isn't just the stuff we can see and hear. It also includes things you might not even realise are affecting us, like unconscious fears or the pressure to act a certain way around certain people. So, if we ever feel a little confused about why we did something, it might be because of the unseen forces buzzing around us in our own personal "zone."

The influential-zone isn't one-sided. You influence it just as much as it influences you. If you suddenly feel nervous during a presentation (change in you), you might start fidgeting or speaking too quickly (change in behaviour). This, in turn, might make the audience feel tense (change in the influential-zone). It's a constant back-and-forth that shapes everything we do.

Our behaviour is influenced not only by internal factors such as motivation or self-control but also by external stimuli and situational cues present in our environment. When this zone becomes cluttered with distractions, interruptions, and confusing instructions, it creates a breeding ground for procrastination.

Two-sided Influence

This avoidance ultimately leads to increased stress and anxiety as deadlines approach. We perceive and interpret our environment through a subjective lens, shaped by our experiences, beliefs, and aspirations

---

If the perceived effort required to complete a task exceeds the perceived rewards or benefits, we may procrastinate to avoid the perceived discomfort or effort associated with the task engagement.

For instance, students, who dream of pursuing a career in writing but find themselves obligated to complete tedious accounting assignments for their course. The misalignment between their passion for writing and the perceived drudgery of accounting creates a psychological discrepancy. Despite understanding the importance of completing the assignments, the perceived effort required outweighs the anticipated rewards. Consequently, students procrastinate, seeking temporary relief from the discomfort of engaging in tasks that diverge from their long-term aspirations.

Discrepancies in the psychological field can manifest as procrastination, as we strive to reconcile our internal desires with external demands.

This is often seen with health goals; we committed to improving our health and fitness by following a structured exercise regimen and adopting a nutritious diet. However, we often find ourselves succumbing to the temptation of unhealthy food choices and sedentary habits due to the convenience and immediate gratification they offer. Despite understanding the long-term benefits of prioritising our health, the perception of the effort required to maintain healthy habits exceeds the perceived rewards, leading to procrastination. We postpone workouts, justify unhealthy eating habits, or engage in avoidance behaviours to evade the discomfort associated with making healthier lifestyle choices.

Creating Influential Zone

To mitigate procrastination tendencies, if we decide to modify our influential zone we can create a more supportive environment for health-promoting behaviours. We can take proactive steps to address our procrastination tendencies and improve our existing routine.

For example, how can you implement this for health goal. Firstly, designate specific times for workouts, blocking off this time in your schedule just as you would for any other important commitment and integrating them into your daily schedule as non-negotiable commitments. By establishing a consistent routine, you create a structured environment that prioritises physical activity.

Next, minimise distractions during your workout sessions by silencing your phone, informing others of your exercise schedule to minimise interruptions, and creating a dedicated workout space free from distractions. This helps maintain focus and concentration during workouts, reducing the likelihood of procrastination.

Furthermore, enhances intrinsic motivation for exercise by connecting it to broader health goals and values. Reflect on the numerous benefits of regular physical activity, such as improved physical fitness, mental well-being, and overall health. By focusing on the long-term rewards of exercise, you will cultivate a sense of purpose and meaning in your fitness pursuits, making it easier to overcome procrastination barriers.

By modifying environmental factors and aligning with task goals, you can overcome procrastination barriers and achieve their desired outcomes with greater efficiency and effectiveness.

If you often find yourself delaying progress and feeling overwhelmed by the project's magnitude. You can proactively modify your psychological field to create a more conducive environment for sustained task engagement. Firstly, designate a specific workspace dedicated solely to the project, free from distractions, fosters concentration and sets the stage for productive work sessions.

Next, break down the project into smaller, manageable tasks with clear milestones and deadlines establishes a structured plan of action, reducing feelings of overwhelm and uncertainty.

Furthermore, cultivate intrinsic motivation by connecting the project to personal and professional aspirations reinforces commitment to its success. Reflecting on the significance of the work and its impact on goals enhances motivation and resilience in the face of challenges or setbacks.

The Power of Choice

Feeling like a cog in the machine can fuel procrastination. By giving choices in how and when we complete tasks, we tap into our natural desire for autonomy and control. This will significantly increase engagement. Schedule tasks for times when you're most productive or when you feel most motivated to tackle them. Offer yourself different ways to approach a task. This could be choosing between digital tools or handwritten notes, working in a specific order or starting with the most challenging aspect.

Understanding the psychological factors that drive productivity and procrastination will provide valuable insights into improving work habits. Comprehending the psychological aspects that influence productivity and procrastination will unlock more effective approaches. Understanding what drives you to complete or avoid tasks will help in devising strategies that align with your natural inclinations and motivations. Such as find a work environment that suits the task and your personal preferences. Some might require a quiet corner, while others might benefit from a collaborative workspace.

By being mindful for your needs and zone, you will shift your focus from the immediate discomfort of a task to the long-term benefits and the satisfaction of accomplishment. This empowers you to overcome procrastination and approach your daily tasks with a sense of agency and fulfilment.

As these changes are implemented, you will begin to notice a shift in mindset and behaviour. By restructuring the psychological field to align with project goals and intentions, a newfound sense of clarity, control, and purpose emerges, empowering you to tackle the project with renewed focus and determination, leading to increased productivity and progress.

Reframing your perspective on these tasks and leveraging our brain's reward system, for example, by giving yourself choices in how you complete them, will make them less overwhelming and ultimately more fulfilling.

Your brain is wired for reward. When you complete a task, you experience a surge of dopamine, a neurotransmitter associated with pleasure and motivation. Procrastination disrupts this cycle, as the avoidance of the task prevents the dopamine reward.

Breaking down large, intimidating projects into smaller, manageable tasks can make them seem less daunting, making it easier to start. Each small task completed provides a dopamine boost, reinforcing the productive behaviour and gradually building momentum toward task completion. Completing smaller steps provides a sense of accomplishment and momentum, making the overall task less daunting.

Making transition easy

Don't wait for the monumental completion to feel good. Celebrate even the small wins of starting a task or completing a sub-step. This reinforces positive behaviour and keeps you motivated. Set up a reward system for completing tasks, especially those you find challenging. This could be a short break, a cup of coffee, or some time spent on a favourite activity. The anticipation of the reward can provide the initial motivation to get started.

Additionally, shifting your focus from the process to the outcome will also help. Visualising the benefits of completing a task will enhance motivation, making the effort seem more worthwhile. This outcome-oriented approach will override the brain's preference for immediate rewards, facilitating engagement with more challenging tasks.

Rewiring the Procrastination Impulse

Procrastination arises when our palaeolithic impulses for immediate gratification overpower our ability to delay gratification for greater long-term gains. But we possess the uniquely human capacity for foresight and mental time travel - to vividly pre-experience rewards before they manifest. By leveraging this strength of consciousness to reprogram our anticipation of fulfilment, we can override our instinctive tendency to procrastinate. We shift our reward system into an efficacy mode geared toward attaining larger, long-horizon wins rather than settling for fleeting pleasures. In doing so, we align our primal drives with our highest aims and unleash our full potential for productive achievement.

Our brains are hardwired to prioritise immediate rewards over long-term benefits - a survival mechanism etched into our evolutionary blueprint. Scrolling through social media feeds, compulsively checking our phones, or indulging in sugary snacks all provide instantaneous hits of pleasure by releasing dopamine, the neurotransmitter governing our reward pathways. Procrastination is often rooted in this innate bias towards instant gratification.

In contrast, tackling challenging tasks or pursuing meaningful goals frequently demands delayed gratification.

The satisfaction of completing a major project, achieving a milestone, or realising a long-held aspiration may be months or even years away. With the rewarding outcome so distant, our primal impulses urge us to choose more immediate "feel-good" options that provide a neurochemical boost in the present moment.

To overcome procrastination, we must consciously rewire our neural circuitry to reverse this destructive tendency. A powerful strategy is to shift our focus away from the arduous process itself and vividly envision the future benefits and rewards of task completion. When we allow our minds to dwell in detail on the positive outcomes awaiting us, we essentially hack our brain's reward system by creating a sense of motivating anticipation.

Instead of ruminating on the drudgery or discomfort of a duty, actively visualise how accomplishing it will propel you towards a long-coveted aim. Imagine the pride of honouring your commitment, the lighter feeling of a burden lifted, or the new opportunities an achievement could unlock. Highlight the ways it will free up time and energy for pastimes you genuinely enjoy. Flesh out this vision with rich details to make it feel tangible and imminent.

By focusing our mental lens not on the means but the meaningful ends, we engage the same neural reward circuitry that usually undermines our efforts. We trick our brains into perceiving the future payoff as an imminent "prize," generating the dopamine-fuelled motivation to persevere through the challenging interim steps. What once triggered procrastination now propels us productively forward.

Of course, human will is inherently limited, and our primal impulses cannot be indefinitely overridden through sheer force of discipline. Balancing periods of intense focus with strategic recovery breaks is essential for sustainable high performance. But by harnessing the power of vividly imagined future rewards, we can consistently outmanoeuvre the procrastination and bring our long-term ambitions into sharper, more motivating focus.

Obstacle 3: Impulses

Impulses are spontaneous, often fleeting urges or desires that arise within individuals' minds. We crave the dopamine rush of a social media notification, the sugary indulgence of a tempting dessert, or the immediate pleasure of a new purchase. However, amidst this constant pursuit of "now," a deeper yearning for fulfilment and long-term meaning can get lost. We seek immediate gratification through distractions. Impulses are driven by instinctual desires, emotions, and conditioned responses, and they can exert a powerful influence on decision-making and behaviour.

The impact of impulses on productivity is multifaceted. On one hand, succumbing to impulsive behaviours can lead to distractions, procrastination, and a loss of focus, ultimately undermining productivity. Constantly checking emails or responding to notifications in response to impulsive urges can disrupt workflow and impede progress on important tasks. On the other hand, not all impulses are inherently detrimental to productivity. In some cases, impulses can serve as valuable signals or cues that prompt individuals to take action or make decisions. For instance, the impulse to take a short break or engage in physical activity can help recharge mental energy and enhance overall productivity in the long run.

Developing awareness of our impulses and their underlying triggers is the first step in managing them effectively. Minimising environmental triggers and distractions will help reduce the occurrence of impulsive behaviours such as creating a dedicated workspace and turning off notifications. We have delved deep in to this in other parts of the book.

Obstacle 4: Fear of Failure

The fear of failing to meet expectations can be deeply unsettling, often manifesting as procrastination or a reluctance to even begin tasks. It stems from a profound dread of making mistakes, falling short of anticipated outcomes, or facing criticism and rejection. This fear is often rooted in concerns about our own competence, worth, or social standing.

When this fear takes hold, it can result in a state of paralysis, rendering us incapable of taking action for fear of making errors or experiencing disappointment. This leads to a plethora of unfinished projects and a stagnation in personal and professional development. Confidence and self-efficacy suffer, causing us to underperform and become excessively risk-averse. In turn, we avoid opportunities for innovation or advancement, fearing potential setbacks or negative feedback.

To break free from the suffocating grip of fear embrace a growth mindset, acknowledging that failure is an indispensable aspect of the learning journey. Rather than viewing challenges as insurmountable obstacles, they should be seen as opportunities for growth, adaptation, and refinement.

Growth mind set is not about reciting positive affirmations, rather it is about acceptance of reality and making necessary changes to overcome obstacles. There is difference between positive affirmation and acceptance. While positive affirmations can be helpful, they often have limited impact compared to the profound transformation that acceptance can bring.

Acceptance is recognising and embracing reality as it is, including acknowledging our limitations, past experiences, and current circumstances. It involves coming to terms with the fact that failure is a natural part of the learning process and that it does not diminish our worth or potential. Instead of fighting against or denying the possibility of failure, acceptance allows us to confront it head-on, thereby reducing the power it holds over us.

Affirmations, while well-intentioned, may fall short in addressing the deep-seated fears and insecurities associated with the fear of failure. Merely repeating positive statements will temporarily boost our confidence, but it will not address the underlying beliefs and emotions that contribute to the fear of failure. Affirmations alone will not provide the depth of insight and self-awareness necessary for meaningful change.

Relying solely on affirmations will lead to a superficial approach to self-improvement, where we attempt to mask our fears with positive statements without truly confronting and addressing them. This will create a disconnect between our outward expressions of confidence and our internal struggles, ultimately hindering genuine growth and development.

In contrast, acceptance encourages us to embrace our vulnerabilities, imperfections, and fears with compassion and courage. It fosters a sense of self-compassion and resilience, allowing us to navigate setbacks and failures with greater ease. By accepting the inevitability of failure as part of the human experience, we can approach challenges with a greater sense of clarity, perspective, and inner peace.

Acceptance opens the door to self-reflection and personal growth, as we gain insights into our fears and motivations. It enables us to cultivate a deeper understanding of self and our relationship with failure, paving the way for more meaningful and sustainable change.

Obstacle 5: Anticipation and Hope

Anticipation and hope are powerful psychological forces that can profoundly shape human behaviour and productivity. While these emotional states are often viewed as positive drivers that motivate us to pursue goals with excitement and purpose, they also possess an insidious potential to distract us and hinder focus if left unchecked.

The experience of anticipating a future reward or achievement can imbue us with a profound sense of motivation. Vividly imagining the fulfilment of a long-sought aspiration ignites a spark of incentive, propelling us into purposeful action to manifest that desired outcome. Similarly, maintaining an optimistic attitude buoyed by hope provides resilience in the face of obstacles and setbacks that might otherwise derail progress.

However, these same psychological experiences can paradoxically undermine productivity when we become overly entranced and preoccupied with future possibilities to the neglect of present-moment tasks. Anticipation morphs into a distraction when our minds fixate on and continuously play out those sought-after future scenarios rather than concentrating on the work required to actualise them.

We may find ourselves indulging in excessive daydreaming about potential rewards, constantly interrupting our workflow to check for status updates, or overplanning and ruminating on each contingency. In doing so, we sacrifice precious attention and energy that could otherwise be channelled into purposeful action and task completion.

The siren song of hope can seduce us into a similar unproductive trance. An unchecked sense of hopefulness can breed false complacency, leading us to adopt an unrealistic, passive expectation that positive outcomes will simply materialise without diligent effort on our part. Rather than rolling up our sleeves to methodically solve problems and take concrete steps toward achievement, we may indulge the fantasy that our aspirations will come to fruition merely through ardent wishing.

To harness the motivational power of anticipation and hope while avoiding their distracting pitfalls, we must cultivate a nuanced awareness. We can revel in visions of future fulfilment, using their inspirational charge to fuel bursts of focused effort toward realising each milestone. However, we must remain anchored in the present, resisting the lure of obsessive fantasies that divert attention from methodical execution.

Similarly, maintaining an optimistic, hopeful perspective is vital for persistence - but not at the cost of falling into passive, wishful thinking. We must harmonise our positive mindset with a proactive, solution-oriented approach rooted in diligent action.

By striking this delicate balance, we transform anticipation and hope from tantalising distractions into potent sources of motivational energy. Harnessed with conscious intention, these forces propel us into highly productive states of rewarding flow - joyfully immersed in the satisfying process of turning our most ambitious dreams into tangible reality.

Obstacle 6: Default Mode

Even with the best of intentions, we all find ourselves periodically lapsing into default mode - that autopilot state where we're simply going through the motions, failing to fully engage with our lives and aspirations. When striving to level up our productivity and flourish in new empowering lifestyles, one of the most formidable obstacles can be the insidious pull of the familiar.

Our psyches develop immense inertia around established habits, routines, and comfort zones. We instinctively cling to the known and resist venturing into new behaviours, no matter how potentially rewarding, because the familiarity of our default patterns feels innately safe. It's easy to find solace in the familiar. Our fear centres sound alarms anytime we attempt deviating from the well-trodden pathways, flooding our minds with discomfort, doubt, and avoidance.

The default mode, that state of autopilot where we navigate through life without truly engaging, can become a pervasive force if left unchecked. It's the path of least resistance, where we follow the grooves worn deep by our past actions and choices. Yet, it's precisely this comfort that often holds us back from reaching our full potential.

The allure of familiarity is powerful, pulling us back into the safety of what we know. Stepping outside of this comfort zone requires courage, for it means confronting the unknown and venturing into uncharted territory. It's in those moments of discomfort, uncertainty, and vulnerability that we find the greatest opportunities for learning and self-discovery. It's where we push past our limits, challenge our assumptions, and expand our horizons.

The prospect of potential failure, rejection, or adverse consequences triggers deeply-wired psychological defences urging us to "play it safe" and avoid putting ourselves in vulnerable positions where we could fall short of success.

Yet the unavoidable truth is that intentionally exposing ourselves to these zones of challenges. Every setback, every stumble, is an opportunity to learn, grow, and evolve. It's through our failures that we gain valuable insights, resilience, and wisdom. By reframing failure as a necessary part of the process, we can free ourselves from the grip of fear and embrace it as a catalyst for growth.

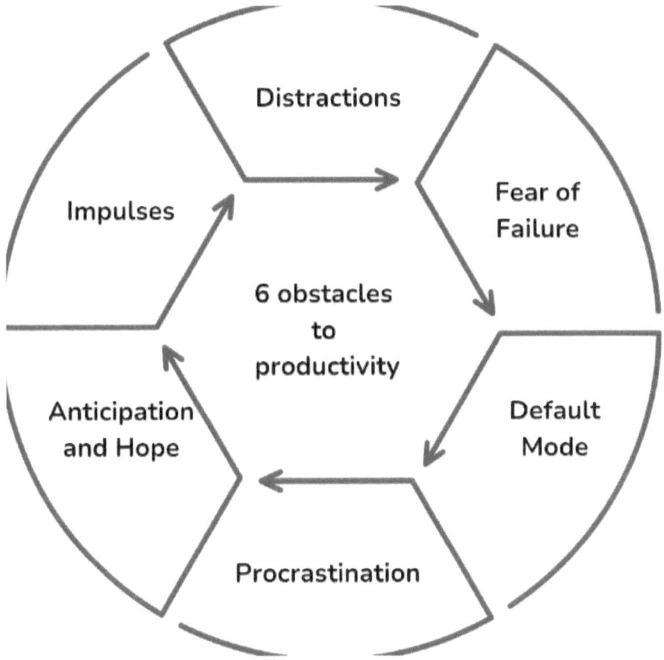

Obstacles to Productivity

PART 2 INFLUENCERS

3 EMOTIONS

"Reason is, and ought only to be, the slave of the passions, and can never pretend to any other office than to serve and obey them."

- David Hume

Emotions act as either a powerful catalyst or a formidable obstacle on our journey towards achieving our goals. Emotions wield significant power, steering our actions or prompting inaction, dictating the course of our lives. Our emotional state can either fuel our productivity or act as a hindrance, influencing our decision-making, concentration, and overall performance.

The oscillation of our emotions can significantly influence our decision-making processes, concentration levels, and overall performance in various aspects of our lives.

Emotions are an undeniable force in our lives, shaping our thoughts, behaviours, and interactions. From the exhilaration of success to the depths of despair, they colour our world and influence how we react. Some emotions, like joy and enthusiasm, propel us forward, while others, like stress and anxiety, can create roadblocks. But emotions are not simply fleeting feelings; they are essential components of our mental processes.

When we find ourselves in a positive emotional state, characterised by feelings of joy, enthusiasm, and optimism, our productivity tends to soar. In this state of emotional buoyancy, we are more likely to approach tasks with a sense of eagerness and determination, fuelled by a deep-seated belief in our abilities and a genuine passion for what we are doing. As a result, our decision-making becomes more decisive and intuitive, our concentration sharpens, and our performance reaches new heights of excellence. Our emotional state can also impact our motivation levels, influencing our willingness to engage with tasks and persevere in the face of challenges. When we are feeling positive and optimistic, we are more likely to approach tasks with a sense of enthusiasm and commitment, driven by a deep-seated desire to succeed.

Conversely, when we are grappling with negative emotions such as stress, anxiety, or despair, our productivity often takes a hit. These emotional burdens can cloud our judgement, causing us to second-guess ourselves, hesitate in our actions, and become paralysed by indecision. Our concentration becomes fragmented, our focus wavers and our performance suffer as a result, leading to a downward spiral of frustration and disillusionment. When negative emotions such as fear or self-doubt creep in, our motivation can wane, making it difficult to summon the energy and determination needed to overcome obstacles and achieve our goals.

Our decisions often serve as the compass guiding our journey. However, beneath the surface of rationality lies a complex interplay of emotions, exerting profound influence over the choices we make. Our feelings shape our decision-making. From the heights of excitement to the depths of uncertainty, each emotion colours our perceptions and propels us towards distinct paths.

When we experience positive emotions such as excitement or hopefulness, our perception of risk may be altered, leading us to underestimate potential negative outcomes or consequences. This can make us more inclined to take risks in pursuit of potential rewards, as the positive emotions associated with the anticipated outcome overshadow concerns about potential risks. For example, someone feeling excited about a new investment opportunity may focus more on the potential gains and less on the associated risks, leading them to make a riskier investment decision.

Decision Compass

Similarly, someone feeling fearful about the uncertain economic climate may choose to delay making significant financial decisions or adopt a more conservative investment strategy to minimise potential losses.

Emotions can also lead to decision-making biases, where our judgements and choices are influenced by our emotional state. For instance, *the optimism bias* characterised by an overestimation of positive outcomes and an underestimation of negative ones. Optimism bias stems from our natural inclination towards positivity and hopefulness. When faced with uncertain or challenging situations, we tend to focus more on potential benefits and favourable outcomes, while downplaying potential risks or negative consequences. One of the mechanisms underlying optimism bias is *selective attention*, where we pay more attention to information that supports our optimistic beliefs while disregarding or minimising contradictory evidence. This selective focus on positive information can reinforce optimistic expectations and contribute to biased decision-making.

Optimism bias is also linked to *self-enhancement motives,* where we have a desire to maintain a positive self-image and perceive themselves in a favourable light. As a result, people may engage in optimistic thinking to protect their self-esteem and boost their confidence, even in the face of uncertainty or adversity. Optimism bias can significantly impact decision-making across various domains, including finance, health, and personal relationships. For example, investors may exhibit optimism bias when evaluating investment opportunities, leading them to overestimate potential returns and underestimate risks. Similarly, individuals may underestimate the likelihood of negative health outcomes or overestimate their ability to achieve unrealistic goals.

Overly optimistic expectations may lead to poor decision-making, increased vulnerability to financial losses, and failure to adequately prepare for potential risks or setbacks.

Recognising the presence of optimism bias is the first step towards mitigating its effects. Encouraging critical thinking, considering alternative viewpoints, and seeking out objective information will help counteract the influence of optimism bias in decision-making. While optimism can be beneficial in many ways, it's essential to remain vigilant and objective in decision-making to avoid the potential pitfalls associated with optimism bias.

Optimism bias can significantly impact productivity, both positively and negatively, depending on how it influences decision-making and behaviour in various contexts. Optimism bias can enhance productivity by fostering confidence, motivation, and resilience. When individuals maintain optimistic beliefs about their abilities and future outcomes, they may approach tasks with enthusiasm and determination, leading to increased productivity and goal achievement. Optimism can also promote a positive mindset, which can be conducive to creativity, problem-solving, and effective collaboration in the workplace.

However, optimism bias can also hinder productivity when it leads to unrealistic expectations and poor decision-making. For example, individuals may underestimate the time and resources required to complete a project, leading to delays and inefficiencies. Similarly, optimism bias can contribute to overconfidence in one's abilities, leading to a reluctance to seek help or feedback, which can impede progress and hinder personal growth.

Our experiences and interactions with the world shape our emotions. For example, the feeling of joy may arise from the experience of pleasure, while the feeling of fear may stem from the perception of danger. These emotions, in turn, colour our experiences, influencing how we interpret and respond to stimuli. A person experiencing fear may perceive a situation as threatening, whereas someone feeling joy may view it as enjoyable.

Emotions also serve as guides to action, prompting us to respond in ways that benefit our well-being. They motivate us to seek pleasure and avoid pain, guiding our actions and decisions. The fear of danger may prompt us to take precautions to ensure our safety, while the desire for pleasure may drive us to pursue opportunities for enjoyment.

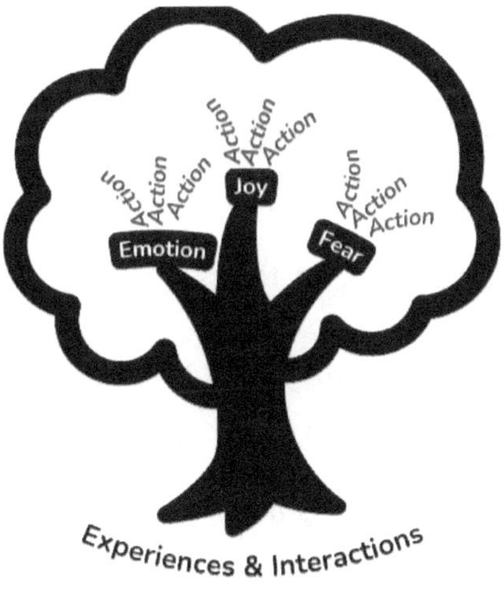

Root to actions

When we experience positive emotions like excitement or happiness, we're more likely to be drawn toward activities that elicit those feelings. For instance, if someone feels excited about travelling to a new destination, this emotion can drive them to plan and pursue that trip. Emotions can shape our desires and goals by affecting what we find rewarding or pleasurable.

Positive emotions such as enthusiasm or determination can provide the energy and drive needed to overcome obstacles and work towards achieving our goals. Conversely, negative emotions like fear or anxiety can also be powerful motivators by prompting us to take action to avoid potential threats or negative outcomes. Emotions play a key role in motivating us to take action.

Some people believe they make decisions solely based on reason, completely devoid of emotions. While they may appear rational on the surface, this is often a case of suppressed emotions. Suppressing emotions doesn't make them disappear – it simply pushes them down. This suppression can be a form of emotion in itself, often driven by a fear of expressing vulnerability or a past experience that conditioned them to avoid certain feelings.

Ignoring or suppressing emotions can be detrimental in the long run. These suppressed emotions can lead to a disconnect between our thoughts and actions, hindering our ability to make sound decisions and achieve our goals. For instance, someone who suppresses their fear of public speaking may avoid opportunities to present their ideas, ultimately hindering their career advancement. Similarly, someone who suppresses feelings of love for a potential partner might miss out on a fulfilling relationship due to a fear of vulnerability or past heartbreak. These suppressed emotions can lead to missed opportunities and a sense of emptiness in various aspects of life.

By understanding the interplay between reason and passion, we can learn to harness the power of our emotions and align them with our long-term goals. If we learn to identify our true passions and align them with long-term goals, we can leverage the power of reason to chart a course toward a more fulfilling life.

Our passions, encompassing emotions, desires, and motivations, are the driving force behind human behaviour. Reason serves these passions, helping us navigate the world to fulfil them. Imagine a delicious cake sitting on a table. Our craving for it wouldn't be created by reason. Reason, however, comes into play when we decide whether to buy the cake, bake it ourselves, or perhaps choose a healthier alternative.

Let's delve deeper into how this interplay between reason and passion affects our pursuit of long-term goals and overall well-being, a concept the Greeks called eudaimonia. Eudaimonia represents a deeper sense of fulfilment that comes from living a meaningful life, pursuing long-term goals, and reaching our full potential.

Decision Making

Emotions are not separate from decision-making; they are integral to it. Recognising and acknowledging the impact of our emotions on our choices is the first step towards mastering productivity. Whether it's the excitement driving us to tackle a new project or the fear holding us back from taking risks, understanding these emotional cues allows us to make more informed decisions.

Optimism bias draws us towards rosy visions of the future, nudging us to embrace positive outcomes while turning a blind eye to potential risks and challenges. This bias is deeply ingrained in human cognition, shaping our expectations and influencing our decisions in subtle yet significant ways. By honing our critical thinking skills, we gain the ability to navigate the complexities of decision-making with greater discernment and objectivity.

It is here that the practice of cultivating finely honed critical thinking skills becomes invaluable. Critical thinking serves as a powerful tool for mitigating the effects of optimism bias and promoting productivity. Critical thinking is the ability to objectively analyse, evaluate, and interpret information and arguments, as well as to assess the validity of assumptions and the soundness of reasoning. It involves actively questioning and examining ideas, evidence, and beliefs, rather than passively accepting them at face value.

We strengthen the ability to scrutinise the assumptions and evidence underlying our beliefs, assessing their validity through rigorous logic rather than blindly clinging to them due to the inertia of hopeful emotion. Critical thinking prompts us to examine our beliefs and assumptions, uncovering the subtle ways in which optimism bias may be influencing our judgements. By rigorously evaluating the evidence supporting optimistic claims, we can discern between wishful thinking and reasoned analysis, making more informed decisions in the process.

Critical thinking enables us to strike a balance between optimism and realism, allowing us to acknowledge the potential benefits of a course of action while also considering the associated risks and challenges. This balanced approach leads to more prudent decision-making and ultimately enhances productivity.

Yet even the most finely honed critical thinking is ultimately incomplete without the complementary awareness that committed mindfulness practice provides. By practising mindfulness, we develop the ability to observe our emotions without being overwhelmed by them. This awareness enables us to respond to situations with greater clarity and intentionality, rather than reacting impulsively based on our emotions. We strengthen our ability to witness the arising and passing of emotions with conducive acceptance, no longer unconsciously identifying with or becoming engulfed by each transitory wave.

Critical thinking provides a rational framework to assess situations objectively, while mindfulness cultivates awareness of our emotions, allowing us to make decisions with clarity and composure. Integrating these two steps empowers us to navigate complex decisions with wisdom and balance.

Decision fatigue is another productivity killer. Minimalism can help by reducing the number of decisions we need to make daily, freeing up mental energy for more important tasks. Create daily and weekly routines to automate small decisions, such as what to wear or what to eat for breakfast. Reduce the range of options when a decision is required to simplify the selection process and speed up action. We have delved into minimalism later in the book.

4 INSTANT GRATIFICATION

When faced with choices that offer immediate rewards or pleasures, we often struggle to resist the allure of instant gratification, even if it comes at the expense of future benefits. This phenomenon, known as temporal discounting, can manifest in various forms of procrastination, from putting off important work in favour of more enjoyable activities to succumbing to distractions that offer instant gratification.

Temporal discounting refers to the tendency of individuals to undervalue future rewards or consequences in comparison to immediate ones. This tendency to prioritise the present over the future can lead to impulsive decision-making and undermine efforts to achieve long-term objectives. The anticipation of reward can lead us to prioritise tasks that offer immediate gratification over those with delayed but more substantial benefits. For example, if given the choice between receiving $100 today or $150 a year from now, many people would choose the $100 today, even though waiting a year would yield a larger financial gain. This preference for immediate gratification over long-term benefits have significant implications for various aspects of life, including personal finance, health behaviours, and decision-making.

We naturally place greater weight on events and outcomes that are closer in time, a phenomenon known as temporal myopia. Consequently, distant rewards or consequences may seem less significant or compelling, leading to prioritise immediate gains. Our brain is wired to seek immediate rewards as a means of satisfying basic needs and desires. Evolutionarily, this preference for immediate gratification served a survival function, ensuring that individuals attended to pressing concerns such as food, shelter, and safety.

Desire for immediate gratification is a powerful force. In today's world, with technology delivering a constant stream of fleeting pleasures, it's easy to get caught up in the pursuit of the "now" at the expense of deeper fulfilment. The purpose of life encompasses more than the pursuit of fleeting pleasures or instant gratification. It involves striving for enduring significance, personal growth, and the realisation of the fullest potential. However, temporal discounting can obscure this broader perspective, leading to prioritise transient experiences or material possessions at the expense of deeper fulfilment and meaning. These experiences of a temporary boost, often leave us feeling unfulfilled and yearning for the next dopamine hit. This focus on the immediate can obscure the bigger picture, leading us to prioritise fleeting pleasures over endeavours that contribute to the lasting significance and personal growth. We are wired for instant gratification, but true fulfilment comes from pursuing long-term goals and personal growth

5 PURSUIT OF FULFILMENT

What truly propels human behaviour and achievement?

Is it the pursuit of external rewards, recognition, and incentives?

Or does a deeper wellspring of motivation arise from the yearning for personal growth and a sense of meaningful contribution?

Human behaviour flows from three main sources: desire, emotion, and knowledge.

-Plato

The ancient philosopher Plato grappled with this profound question of the underlying drivers of human conduct. In his celebrated work Phaedrus, he put forth the allegory of the charioteer to illustrate the eternal interplay between reason, emotion, and appetite within the human psyche.

Plato envisioned the human soul as a charioteer valiantly steering a chariot propelled by two powerful winged horses locked in a perennial tug-of-war. One horse, embodying our noblest virtues and rational capacities, yearns to ascend toward the idealised realms of knowledge, wisdom, and self-actualisation. The other, unruly steed personifies our base impulses - the primal cravings for gratification, status, and immediate pleasures that frequently lure us off our highest course.

However, if the charioteer loosens the reins and succumbs to the unrestrained pulls of appetite, the entire enterprise veers into chaos and distraction - mired in aimless pursuits of instant gratification devoid of deeper meaning or lasting satisfaction.

The allegory reveals that the path to human flourishing lies not in the ruthless suppression of emotion and natural desires, but rather in cultivating the wisdom to harmonise and integrate them with our highest rational capacities. When reason, emotion, and appetite collaborate in balanced synchronicity, we experience a transcendent state of flow - joyfully engaged in activities that meaningfully express our authentic talents and values.

We can channel our emotions and desires into productive pursuits, utilising them as fuel to propel ourselves towards personal fulfilment. achieving our highest potential requires not just reason, but also a harmonious integration of all aspects of the human experience. By recognising the complex interplay between these forces, we gain a deeper understanding of ourselves and our motivations. This self-awareness empowers us to make conscious choices and navigate the internal chariot race with greater skill, achieving a more fulfilling and meaningful life.

Many times, we struggle to define what truly matters to us and set meaningful goals that resonate with our authentic selves. Without a clear sense of purpose, we may find ourselves drifting aimlessly, lacking direction and motivation. Taking the time to reflect on our values, passions, and aspirations helps us gain clarity and purpose in our lives.

"The function of man is to live a certain kind of life, and this activity implies a rational principle, and the function of a good man is the good and noble performance of these, and if any action is well performed it is performed in accord with the appropriate excellence: if this is the case, then happiness turns out to be an activity of the soul in accordance with virtue."

Aristotle

Centuries later, philosopher Aristotle furthered the exploration into what constitutes a life well-lived. In his seminal Nicomachean Ethics, he posited that all human behaviours arise from a singular driving motivation: the desire to experience "eudaimonia" - often translated as happiness or human flourishing, but more aptly understood as the profound sense of fulfilment that arises from living life in alignment with reason and realising one's highest potentials as a human being.

Aristotle

Every action is driven by the pursuit of some good, and the highest good, which is desired for its own sake, is what he called the "chief good." This chief good, he identified as eudaimonia, often translated as happiness or flourishing. However, eudaimonia is not simply feeling content or pleased. It's about living a life that fulfils one's potential as a human being, living well in accordance with human nature.

Humans are distinguished from other animals by their rationality. Therefore, the good life for a human involves the life of the mind. Aristotle identified different ways of living, the life of pleasure, the political life focused on civic virtue, and the contemplative life focused on reason. While acknowledging the importance of each and its value. Aristotle put across his thought that the contemplative life is the highest form of flourishing because it involves the exercise of reason, our defining characteristic.

Aristotle contended that this state of eudaimonia could not be achieved through the myopic pursuit of pleasure, wealth or individualistic pursuits alone. Rather, true fulfilment emerges through consciously devoting oneself to activities that harmonise the physical, emotional, and rational dimensions of our nature - engaging our ethics, our civic virtues, and above all, the rigorous application of our uniquely human faculty for logic, contemplation, and wonder.

While recognising the intrinsic values of pleasure, prosperity and passion, Aristotle positioned the "contemplative life" dedicated to the earnest pursuit of knowledge and truth as the pinnacle of human striving and the ultimate path to eudaimonia. For it is through the diligent exercise of our rational capacities that we most fully express our essential human nature and elevate our consciousness to transcendent planes of meaning and self-actualisation.

So how can we, in our frenetic modern age, cultivate the conditions for purposeful flourishing? The path begins with a profound shift in perspective - transcending pursuits of mere busyness, shallow accomplishments or temporary pleasures. We must realign our energy and attention toward activities that nourish our souls and facilitate our evolution as conscious beings.

The first step is to shift our focus from instant gratification to activities that contribute to long-term goals and personal growth. This doesn't mean eliminating all pleasure; it's about achieving a balance. True productivity lies not in doing more tasks but in doing the right tasks well, those that contribute most to our overall well-being and fulfilment

6 PEER PRESSURE

Social interactions and expectations often exert a significant influence on our emotional well-being. Social pressure comes through the expectations and norms imposed by society, workplaces, and even personal relationships.

The nuances between social pressures, emotional drain and social intelligence have their collective influence on our ability to perform.

The desire to conform, excel, and be accepted can create an undercurrent of stress that saps our emotional reserves.

When we continually adjust our behaviours, suppress our authentic selves, or strive to meet unrealistic standards, the resultant emotional drain can leave us depleted, affecting our focus and energy.

Soren Kierkegaard a Danish philosopher is regarded as the father of existentialism. The groundwork for existentialism laid by Kierkegaard's philosophy is the concept of subjective truth that is deeply personal and rooted in individual experience rather than objective, universal principles.

External factors such as social norms, expectations, and conventional morality are given more importance than individual freedom and personal responsibility. Kierkegaard believed that individuals should strive to live authentic lives, guided by their inner convictions and values rather than conforming blindly to external standards.

He argued against the conformity that comes with blindly adhering to societal expectations, advocating instead for a life lived in accordance with one's own inner truth and values.

Most people are subjective toward themselves and objective toward all others, frightfully objective sometimes-but the task is precisely to be objective toward oneself and subjective toward all others. They are objective in the wrong place, because they allow themselves everything, and subjective in the wrong place, because when the slightest thing happens to them they promptly become subjectively affected.

Soren Kierkegaard

In a world where social norms and conventions often dictate behaviour, we may feel compelled to conform to external standards, sacrificing our values and desires in the process. Resist this pressure and instead embrace our inner convictions. By aligning our actions with authentic selves, we cultivate a sense of integrity and self-respect, which are essential for maintaining mental well-being.

Your truth may differ from societal norms and expectations. By acknowledging and honouring own truth, we can cultivate a sense of autonomy empowering us to make decisions that are in line with our personal values and aspirations.

Emotional Drain

The emotional drain resulting from chronic social pressure significantly impair life goals. When our mental energy is consumed by anxiety, stress, and self-doubt, there's less capacity for creativity, problem-solving, and focused work. The preoccupation with social judgement leads to decision fatigue, tempers in risk-taking ability, and a tendency to avoid challenging tasks, all of which stifle personal and professional growth.

Dealing with peer pressure encompasses how we interact and communicate with others. Effective communication, setting clear boundaries, mastering the art of delegation and saying no are essential skills for maintaining productivity within the context of our relationships, both personal and professional. Effective communication is the cornerstone of productive relationships. It involves being clear, concise, and direct to minimise misunderstandings and the need for time-consuming clarifications.

Delegating tasks and asserting your boundaries by saying no are powerful tools for maintaining productivity within our team. Delegating allows to concentrate on tasks that are best suited to our skills and align with our priorities, thereby ensuring that our time is utilised effectively. Identifying tasks that others can handle and providing clear instructions and expectations fosters a culture of trust and collaboration within our team. Delegation not only frees up our time but also contributes to the professional development of our colleagues, empowering them to take on new challenges and expand their skills. Recognise that time is a limited resource. Politely declining requests that don't align with your priorities or current workload is essential for maintaining focus and productivity.

However, in the process of delegation, you may encounter peer pressure from colleagues who expect you to take on more tasks or responsibilities than you can handle. This pressure can stem from various sources, such as a desire to meet tight deadlines or a fear of letting down team members. While it's important to be a team player and contribute to shared goals, it's equally vital to recognise your limitations and maintain a healthy work-life balance.

When faced with peer pressure to take on additional tasks, it's essential to assess the impact on workload and priorities. Communicate openly with colleagues about existing commitments and bandwidth, explaining why there is a need to decline certain requests. By setting clear boundaries and managing expectations effectively, you can navigate peer pressure without compromising your productivity or well-being.

Furthermore, use delegation as a strategic tool to distribute workload more evenly within the team, thereby alleviating the pressure on individual team members. Involving others in the decision-making process and empowering them to take ownership of tasks, foster a sense of collective responsibility and collaboration.

7 ORGANISED LIFESTYLE

The human desire for order is an ancient one. From the meticulously planned cities of Mesopotamia to the meticulously labelled spice racks of modern kitchens, a sense of organisation fosters not just efficiency, but also a sense of calm. This is particularly true within our workspaces, those physical manifestations of our intellectual pursuits. A cluttered desk, overflowing with forgotten coffee cups and dog-eared to-do lists, creates a visual cacophony that can impede focus and hinder productivity. A cluttered workspace becomes a mental burden, constantly vying for our attention. Yet path to an organised workspace is not as daunting as it may seem.

The Artful Declutter

The first step on this journey is the act of decluttering. Imagine your workspace as a bustling marketplace, once vibrant but now overflowing with forgotten trinkets and extraneous wares. A thorough decluttering session is akin to a market clear-out, where you, the discerning stallholder, must assess the value of each item. Does it serve a purpose in your daily working life? Does it spark a flicker of inspiration or a surge of joy? If not, consider parting ways with the item. Donate it to a worthy cause, recycle it responsibly, or, if absolutely necessary, consign it to the bin. Remember, a workspace should be a source of inspiration, not a museum of forgotten tasks.

Categorisation and Containment

Once the initial decluttering wave has subsided, it's time to establish a system of categorisation. Group your remaining items into logical categories: office supplies, essential documents, reference materials, etc. Create designated homes for each category. This not only creates a visual map of your workspace, but also fosters a sense of order and control. Imagine a meticulously labelled library, where each book resides on its designated shelf, waiting to be discovered. Your workspace, too, can become a haven of organised knowledge, with every essential item readily at your fingertips.

Optimising Your Space

Finally, consider how you can optimise your workspace for maximum productivity and focus. Embrace natural light, a potent ally that can banish the shadows of fatigue and stimulate concentration. A comfortable chair, a personal touch like a favourite mug or a framed photograph, can all contribute to a workspace that feels not just organised, but also welcoming and inspiring.

An organised space is not just an end goal, but a foundation for a more peaceful and ultimately, a more fulfilling life. Disorganisation can lead to wasted time searching for information or resources, missed deadlines, and increased stress. Developing systems and routines for organised life helps us streamline our workflows and enhance productivity.

While organisation is a powerful tool, it's important to remember that perfection is not the goal. Embrace a sense of relaxed order, where functionality and comfort reign supreme. Don't get bogged down in the minutiae of placement, a well-loved space will naturally show some signs of life. Focus on creating a space that sparks joy allows you to thrive, not one that feels like a museum exhibit.

Cultivating Order in Your Mind Space

We've explored the transformative power of decluttering and organising your physical space. But what about the space between your ears? Our minds, too, can become cluttered with unfinished tasks, swirling anxieties, and a never-ending to-do list. This mental clutter can be just as detrimental to productivity and peace of mind as a messy desk.

The first step to mental organisation is to capture the chaos. Our brains are excellent at generating ideas and tasks, but not so great at holding onto them. To prevent your mind from becoming a swirling vortex of to-dos, grab a notebook, a digital to-do list app, or even a trusty scrap of paper. Jot down everything – errands, appointments, project ideas, that nagging voice reminding you to call your Auntie. Externalise this mental chaos, creating a visual roadmap of all that needs to be done.

Now that you have a clear picture of your mental landscape, it's time to prioritise. Not all tasks are created equal. Delegate or eliminate less crucial tasks to free up mental space for those that truly matter. Learning to decline is a crucial skill for mental organisation. We often feel obligated to say "yes" to every request, even when it adds to our already overflowing mental plate. Remember, it's perfectly acceptable to say no to protect your time and energy. By politely declining tasks that don't align with your priorities, you create space for the things that truly matter.

When you have completed task, celebrate the feeling of completion. Ticking completed tasks off your list provides a powerful sense of accomplishment and helps to clear mental clutter. Take a moment to acknowledge your progress, no matter how small. This act of acknowledging completion can motivate you to tackle the next item on your list and keep your mental space feeling organised and clear.

Simplify Your Tech Life

We've explored the art of taming the physical realm and cultivating order within your mind. But the digital frontier that ever-expanding landscape of emails, overflowing inboxes, and a seemingly endless stream of notifications can also become a battleground for mental clarity.

The first step to digital decluttering is tackling the dreaded inbox avalanche. Imagine your inbox as a bustling marketplace, overflowing with forgotten messages and extraneous solicitations. Employ a ruthless filtering system, deleting irrelevant emails and unsubscribing from unwanted newsletters. Consider using folders or labels to categorise remaining messages, creating a sense of order and allowing you to locate specific information with ease.

The incessant barrage of notifications from social media applications, news alerts, and email updates can be a significant source of digital clutter. Silence the notification tyrants by customising your settings. Turn off unnecessary alerts and schedule dedicated times to check your email and social media. This will help you regain control of your attention and prevent constant interruptions.

Our digital world often bombards us with a multitude of tasks and demands. Utilise tools to prioritise these tasks. Schedule dedicated time slots for tackling emails, responding to messages, and completing online projects. This fosters a sense of structure and prevents you from feeling overwhelmed by the digital deluge.

Just as our bodies crave physical rest, our minds also require periods of digital detachment. Schedule regular digital detox times when you completely disconnect from your devices. This allows your brain to process information, recharge, and return to the digital world feeling refreshed and focused.

A well-organised digital environment empowers you to reclaim control of your time and attention, allowing you to navigate the digital world with greater efficiency and peace of mind.

Power of Planning

Schedule regular planning sessions, daily, monthly and yearly. Use this time to prioritise tasks, set realistic goals, and create a to-achieve-list that outlines the steps needed to achieve them. Dedicate each day's first 10 minutes to planning your day and review your day at the end. Schedule a monthly planning session to delve deeper into your goals and aspirations. Review your progress towards your long-term objectives and identify any adjustments needed. Break down larger projects into smaller, monthly milestones to maintain momentum and avoid feeling overwhelmed.

Dedicate time at the beginning of each year to set ambitious yet achievable goals. This could involve crafting a vision board, outlining your aspirations in various aspects of life. Break down these yearly goals into actionable steps, assigning them to specific quarters and months throughout the year.

By implementing this multi-layered approach to prioritisation and planning, you'll gain a holistic perspective on your time. Daily planning sessions ensure you tackle the most important tasks each day, while monthly and yearly reviews keep you focused on your long-term objectives. Effective prioritisation and planning empower you to navigate the whirlwind of daily life with focus, clarity, and a sense of accomplishment.

With organised systems in place, we can move seamlessly from one task to the next without wasting time searching for information or resources. When we're not bogged down by disorganisation, we can focus our energy on the tasks that truly matter, leading to increased productivity and a greater sense of accomplishment. A well-organised life fosters a sense of calm and control. Knowing where things are and having a plan in place reduces stress and allows us to approach challenges with a clear head.

Staying Organised

Staying organised is not just about having a neat desk or tidy workspace; maintaining organisation in our surroundings and routines can have profound effects on our cognitive abilities and emotional well-being.

One of the most significant advantages of staying organised is the significant reduction in cognitive load. This term refers to the amount of mental effort our brains exert to process information and complete tasks. Imagine our brains as busy workspaces. When our physical environment or digital world is cluttered and disorganised, it's like having papers scattered everywhere in our workspace. Sorting through the mess to find what we need takes time and energy.

In the same way, a cluttered environment bombards our brains with irrelevant information. We have to work harder to filter out the distractions and focus on the specific task at hand. This constant filtering process increases our cognitive load, leading to mental fatigue. We might feel sluggish, have difficulty concentrating, and even experience decision-making paralysis.

The magic of staying organised lies in its ability to streamline our mental workspace. By organising our physical space, like decluttering our desk or room, and organising our digital files, we eliminate the visual clutter that consumes our brain's resources. With less irrelevant information to process, our cognitive load is reduced. This allows our brains to function more efficiently and effectively. It's like having a clean and organised workspace – we can find what we need quickly and focus our energy on the task at hand, accomplishing more with less mental strain.

Imagine we're trying to write a report. In a cluttered environment, it's like having papers, books, and half-eaten biscuits piled on our desks. Every time we look up from our writing, our gaze lands on something distracting. We might spend a few seconds (or minutes) trying to decipher what it is, even if it has nothing to do with our report. This constant filtering uses up our mental energy.

Now, imagine a clean desk with only our laptop, notepad, and a pen. There's nothing to distract us visually, so our brains can focus solely on writing the report. We'll find ourselves getting into a flow state, completing the task more efficiently and with less mental fatigue.

By staying organised, we create a similar environment for our brains, both physically and digitally. This allows us to tap into our full potential and achieve more with less mental strain.

When our surroundings are chaotic and cluttered, it can trigger feelings of overwhelm and anxiety. Chronic stress can have detrimental effects on our physical and mental health, leading to fatigue, decreased immunity, and impaired cognitive function. By maintaining an organised environment, we create a sense of calm and control, reducing stress levels and promoting overall well-being.

Disorganisation, like a messy desk overflowing with forgotten coffee cups and crumpled to-do lists, has a ripple effect throughout our lives.

It can lead to:

Wasted Time

Imagine spending precious minutes (or even hours) frantically searching for a misplaced document or the perfect file you know you downloaded somewhere. Disorganisation forces us to retrace our steps, wasting valuable time that could be spent on actually getting things done.

Missed Deadlines

When everything feels chaotic, deadlines can easily sneak up on us. Disorganised workflows make it difficult to track progress and prioritise tasks, leading to a constant scramble to meet deadlines at the last minute.

Increased Stress

The constant feeling of being behind or overwhelmed by clutter can be a major source of stress. Disorganisation creates a sense of uncertainty and disarray, making it difficult to relax and focus on the task at hand.

PART 3 PREPARATION

8 LIVING ON PURPOSE

The mystery of human existence lies not in just staying alive, but in finding something to live for.

Fyodor Dostoevsky

Purpose provides the motivation and direction for how we spend our precious time and energy. It defines what matters most to us and steers us towards living more intentionally. Without a driving purpose, our days can feel rudderless, constantly reacting to urgencies and distractions rather than proactively investing in what's truly meaningful.

To unlock our productivity potential, we must first uncover our "why" - the core values, goals, and sources of fulfilment that resonate most deeply. Discovering our unique purpose is an illuminating process of self-discovery. It provides the inspirational spark that propels us into action and gives our productivity meaningful direction.

With our purpose identified as our North Star, we can then engage in productive planning. Planning is the bridge between our noble intentions and tangible results. It's the mechanism that translates our big picture vision into bite-sized, actionable steps.

With our purpose firmly ingrained and meticulous planning in place, we can finally experience true productivity. We shift from reactively completing tasks to proactively advancing the endeavours that resonate with our deepest beliefs and propel us towards our vision.

Purposeful productivity is about being intentional with how we invest one of life's most precious resources - our time and energy. It ensures we don't get bogged down in the trivial many at the cost of losing sight of the vital few activities and goals that unlock our fullest potential and impact.

When we harmonise our daily productivity with our life's purpose, we find deeper fulfilment and motivation. We upgrade from simply checking boxes to doing work that adds value and creates positive ripples. Not all planning is created equal.

The difference between merely organising tasks and orchestrating a purposeful plan can be the decisive factor between mediocrity and excellence.

Purposeful planning is the art of intentional productivity, where every action is aligned with a deeper sense of purpose, leading to meaningful and impactful outcomes.

What Is Purposeful Planning?

Purposeful planning transcends conventional planning by infusing goals and tasks with intentionality and alignment to our core values and long-term objectives. It's about asking the "why" behind our actions and ensuring that every step you take is moving us closer to our larger mission. This method not only enhances productivity but also ensures that our efforts are fulfilling and sustainable. By understanding the purpose behind our tasks, we gain unparalleled clarity and focus. This prevents distractions and enhances our ability to prioritise effectively. When we see the connection between our daily tasks and our overarching goals, we remain engaged and driven.

How to Implement Purposeful Planning

Take the time to thoughtfully consider both your ultimate desired destinations and the incremental milestones that will mark progress along the way.

Step 1: Define Your Purpose

The foundation of purposeful planning lies in understanding your purpose. Reflect on your core values, passions, and long-term objectives. Ask yourself:

- What are my core values?
- What are my long-term goals?
- What legacy do I want to leave?

Write down your purpose statement, which will serve as your guiding star. A vision board is a powerful visual tool that brings your goals and dreams to life. By showcasing your aspirations through images, quotes, and affirmations, it keeps you inspired and focused on your path to success.

Step 2: Set SMART Goals

Translate your purpose into Specific, Measurable, Achievable, Relevant, and Time-bound (SMART) goals. Ensure these goals align with your purpose statement. This helps in creating a roadmap that is both actionable and aligned with your core mission.

Step 3: Break Down Goals into Tasks

Decompose your SMART goals into manageable tasks. Each task should have a clear objective and deadline. Use backward planning, starting from the end goal and working backwards to ensure that every task is a stepping stone towards your larger objectives.

Step 4: Prioritise with Purpose

Not all tasks are created equal. Use prioritisation to ensure you are focusing on what truly matters. Evaluate tasks based on their alignment with your purpose and their impact on your goals.

Step 5: Schedule with Intention

Design a schedule that reflects your priorities and purpose. Allocate time blocks for high-impact tasks during your peak productivity periods. Ensure your schedule is flexible enough to accommodate unexpected changes while remaining focused on your purpose.

Step 6: Review and Reflect

Regularly review your progress and reflect on your alignment with your purpose. Set aside time weekly and monthly to assess your achievements, adjust your plans, and ensure you are on track. This reflective practice ensures continuous alignment and improvement. Journaling helps in clarifying thoughts, tracking progress, and staying connected with your purpose. Maintain a journal to document your purpose, goals, progress, and reflections.

9 MINDSET

At the heart of mastering true productivity lies not merely adopting refined practices, but undergoing a profound shift in our fundamental mindset, the core beliefs, perspectives, and emotional tendencies that underpin our actions. No matter how sophisticated the tactics and tools we employ, they are bound to falter in the face of deeply ingrained self-limiting assumptions, fear-driven conditioning, and emotionally reactive patterns.

To consistently reach new levels of flourishing productivity, we must adopt an attitude of intentional growth, a disposition that embraces each challenge as an opportunity for expansion rather than something to evade or shrink from. This journey towards personal mastery commences with making peace with the perpetual process of self-deconstruction and reinvention.

One of the most formidable obstacles to unlocking new realms of productivity is the fixed belief in the immutability of our qualities and abilities. Those absorbed by this mindset instinctively shun situations that might expose weaknesses or invite critical evaluations, as such scenarios threaten their deeply entrenched identity-level attachments. When confronted with setbacks or the prospect of arduous effort, they retreat into self-preservation mode, conjuring up self-handicapping excuses, shirking responsibility, or dismissing endeavours as inconsequential. Their fear of vulnerability and damage to self-image perpetually curtails their potential for growth.

Conversely, those who embrace change and adaptability welcome challenges, persist through obstacles, and regard failures not as roadblocks, but as opportunities to refine their skills. They possess a profound understanding that qualities can be nurtured through perseverance, and they perceive struggles as inevitable milestones rather than dead ends. Their sense of self derives not from proving superiority, but from the inherently rewarding journey of perpetual evolution and expansion.

Those gripped by a fixed belief system instinctively view productivity as a means of showcasing their superiority and defending an image. Conversely, those who embrace growth recognises productivity as a vehicle for continual learning, refinement, and contribution. Tools and systems become enablers of creative expression and self-actualisation rather than badges of achievement.

Authentic growth demands venturing beyond the boundaries of our competence and certitude on a regular basis. It entails embracing the discomfiting vulnerability of being a perpetual "not-knowing," time and again, as we venture into unfamiliar territories. A growth-oriented mindset regards each uncharted realm not as a threat to evade or a power struggle to conquer, but as another fertile ground for insight and inspiration to flourish. It greets each new opportunity for self-transcendence with curiosity and excitement.

Embracing this disposition requires shedding the egoic shackles that bind us to the well-worn pathways of past conditioning. It involves relinquishing attachments to performances, titles, and accolades. We release the ego's incessant need to solidify its existence through ceaseless demonstrations of significance and instead take refuge in the liberating realisation that we are eternally works-in-progress.

Within this fluidity, we find ourselves anchored in the unshakable essence of pure being, no longer fixated on maintaining rigid self-structures, but rather revelling in the freedom of unbridled exploration and fresh expression. Failures and setbacks cease to unsettle us, for our self-worth is no longer entwined with narrow notions of achievement. Instead, we remain open to the wisdom inherent in each experience, distilling the rejuvenating insights awaiting integration.

Hand-in-hand with the vulnerability of not-knowing is the art of non-attachment, accepting each circumstance and outcome with equanimity. This is not to be confused with emotional bypassing or apathy, but rather a instinctual freedom born of no longer unconsciously resisting the unfolding of reality. The mindset of growth recognises that much of our suffering stems not from external events, but from the inner narratives and created opinions labelled onto them.

Just as a skilled surfer learns to attune to the present rhythms of the ocean rather than rigidly imposing their will upon it, we too can practice surrendering to the natural ups and downs of our lives, neither resisting the change nor clinging to artificial stability. This allows us to reprogram our conditioned reflex to push against difficulties and evade unfamiliar territories. We cease waging futile battles to impose fixed ideals on inherently fluid existences. Anxiety, frustration, and non-stop reflection dissolve as we greet each moment with tranquil presence.

Of course, non-attachment is not a passive resignation, but rather the cultivation of skilful responsiveness. Just as a masterful surfer makes calculated adjustments to navigate ever-shifting conditions, those embodying a growth mindset act with intention while flowing through the organic transitions of life. Obstacles become opportunities for pivoting towards new possibilities. Dead-ends reveal themselves as invitations to reaffirm our deeper purpose and redirect our trajectory. Each fractal of experience is welcomed as a clue towards exponential expansion.

It may be tempting to idealise growth and equate a productive mindset with a perpetual state of boundless confidence, unwavering determination, and inexhaustible vitality. However, even among those who rigorously cultivate their psychology for expansion, moments of inner resistance, self-doubt, fear, and lethargy will inevitably arise. These are not flaws to be eradicated, but the very base that provides traction for our continual evolution.

What sets apart those who consistently transcend their limitations from those who stagnate is the emotional transformation they bring to the struggles integral in the journey of mastery. This alchemical capacity arises from the fundamental recognition that all internal experiences are transitory, that no emotional state, however intense or deeply ingrained, must solidify into a permanent aspect of our identity. We liberate ourselves from the compulsion to equate passing feelings with immutable truths about our capabilities or self-worth.

A fleeting wave of nervousness or transient sense of misery does not necessitate adopting a narrative of being "unprepared," "incapable," or "off-course." Those committed to personal mastery simply observe these experiences with compassionate acceptance, allowing them to arise, play out, and dissipate of their own accord. Fear transmutes into wisdom, and lethargy into insight on optimising resource allocation. Our very struggles become the fertile soil for exponential growth.

At its essence, cultivating a mindset aligned with continuous growth and self-expansion involves embracing the ever-emergent and fundamentally improvisational nature of existence itself.

We recognise that there is no static "end state" where everything is finally resolved, no ultimate finish line heralding the completion of our evolution. Life itself is a dynamic, fractal unfolding of creative becoming.

Productivity emerges as a spontaneous expression, not as something coerced through sheer effort and willpower. From this perspective, the linear narratives our minds concoct about "paths" to "achieving goals" dissolve into transparent visions. Suddenly, we find ourselves able to rest in the inherent richness of each present moment, attending only to what demands our focused attention and energy in that instant. We no longer demand that life adhere to arbitrary timelines or prescribed ideals. Instead, we respond to what is arising and pivot as necessary.

The fluidity itself becomes the path.

Within this paradigm, "productivity" naturally evolves into the seamless integration of being and expressing in alignment with the highest universal patterns of order. Conventional notions of "work-life balance" give way to a holistic understanding of our entire existence as a pristine manifestation of unobstructed contribution. Our focus expands beyond narrow self-interest to encompass the intentional cultivation of environments that evoke states of flow not only within ourselves but also in the broader collective.

The structures and systems we create are not designed merely to optimise individual "success," but to unleash the infinite scalability of our most harmonious collaborative resonance. We redefine productivity not as a metric, but as the ongoing refinement of our capacity to authentically express and contribute.

10 HABIT

Behaviour is determined by its consequences.

B. F. Skinner

Habits are the brain's way of automating repeated behaviours to save energy. This automation allows us to perform many activities without conscious thought, from brushing our teeth to driving a car. The power of habit lies in this ability to free up our mental resources so we can focus on more complex tasks. When positive behaviours become habitual, life becomes less about exerting willpower and more about following the natural flow of our daily routines. When we understand how habits are formed, how to break old habits and build new, life will be simpler

Power of Habits

Habits, whether they be daily routines, behavioural patterns, or thought processes, shape our lives in profound ways, influencing our success, happiness, and overall well-being. Yet, establishing and maintaining new habits can often be a challenging endeavour, requiring patience, perseverance, and a clear understanding of the psychological principles that govern human behaviour.

Edward L. Thorndike is known for his pioneering work in the early 20th century, particularly his research on learning and the development of the "law of effect." Thorndike's, work emphasises the power of consequences in shaping behaviour. If we consistently receive a reward after performing an action, we're likely to associate that action with the reward and continue doing it. Conversely, if we're consistently punished instead of rewarded, we're likely to avoid that action in the future. The more frequently the action and its effect are connected, the stronger the bond between them becomes. For this bond to form, whether it's a positive or negative effect, repetition is key.

Imagine you're a busy professional who struggles with procrastination when it comes to completing your work projects. Despite your best intentions, you often find yourself putting off important tasks until the last minute, leading to stress, anxiety, and subpar results. The first step to overcome this is to recognise the need for change, overcome your procrastination habit and develop more productive work habits.

Favourable stimulus

Begin by identifying the specific behaviours you want to reinforce, such as starting work on your projects earlier and staying focused throughout the process. Set up a reward system for yourself, where you earn points or tokens for each hour of focused work completed without procrastinating. These points can be exchanged for small rewards, such as a coffee break, a walk outside, or a leisure activity you enjoy.

In addition to positive reinforcement, create an environment that supports your productivity and makes it easier to stay focused on your tasks. Set up an "anti-procrastination zone" in your workspace, free from distractions such as social media, email notifications, and unnecessary clutter. By removing these aversive stimuli, you create a conducive environment for concentration and productivity.

Removal of an unfavourable stimulus

Whenever you catch yourself procrastinating or delaying work unnecessarily, impose a consequence such as delaying your break time, forfeiting a reward, or setting a timer for an additional 15 minutes of work before taking a break.

Identify potential distractions or time-wasting activities that you indulge in when procrastinating, such as checking social media or watching videos online. Whenever you catch yourself engaging in these activities instead of working, impose a consequence such as temporarily blocking access to distracting websites or limiting your screen time until you complete your work.

B F Skinner was an American Phycologist, social philosopher and behaviourist extended the work on Law of effect. He developed a theory of operant conditioning. Theory focuses on how behaviour is shaped by its consequences. Theory deals with voluntary responses.

By leveraging the principles of reinforcement, punishment, and extinction, we can effectively shape our habits, replacing old, unproductive patterns with new, positive ones that align with our goals and aspirations.

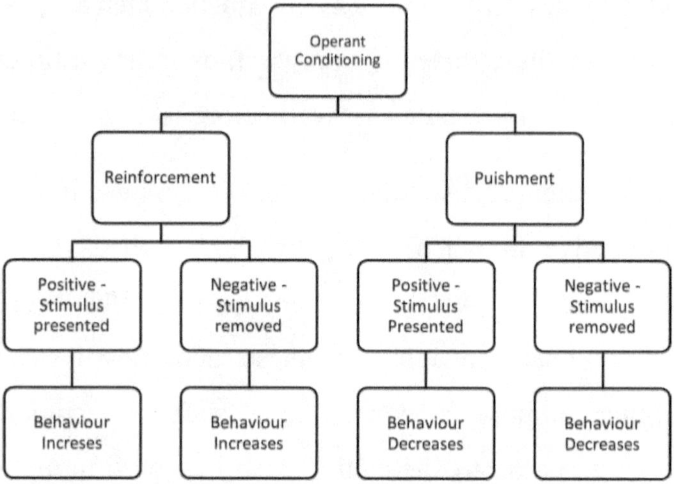

B F Skinner Operant Conditioning Model

Reinforcement is the process by which a behaviour is strengthened or weakened based on its consequences. It's about the consequences that follow your actions. Positive reinforcement involves the addition of a desirable stimulus following a behaviour, increasing the likelihood of that behaviour recurring in the future. For example, receiving praise or rewards for completing a task can serve as positive reinforcement, reinforcing the habit of task completion.

Imagine getting a pat on the back for completing a tough task. That's positive reinforcement! It involves adding something pleasant after a desired behaviour, making you more likely to repeat it. Think of a treat after finishing a project, or a relaxing bath after tackling your to-do list.

Negative reinforcement, on the other hand, involves the removal of an aversive stimulus following a behaviour, also increasing the likelihood of that behaviour recurring. Negative reinforcement isn't about punishment, it's about removing something unpleasant. For instance, removing a nagging alarm by waking up promptly in the morning can serve as negative reinforcement, reinforcing the habit of waking up early. Hitting the snooze button silences the annoying alarm, but you also miss out on precious sleep! However, silencing the alarm by waking up on time reinforces the habit of early mornings.

Using reinforcement effectively is aligning rewards and consequences with your desired behaviours. Like a mental handshake, consistent rewards for good habits and removing the downsides of bad habits strengthen the neural pathways in your brain. Over time, these habits become automatic, making them easier to maintain.

To build effective habits using reinforcement, identify and implement appropriate rewards and consequences that align with our desired behaviours.

While reinforcement focuses on increasing the likelihood of desired behaviours, punishment aims to decrease the likelihood of undesired behaviours through the application of aversive consequences.

Punishment aims to discourage unwanted behaviours by making them unpleasant. There are two main types:

Positive Punishment

Adding something unpleasant after a bad habit. Imagine the frustration of a messy room leading to lost phone privileges. This unpleasant consequence discourages repeating messy behaviour. Positive punishment involves the addition of an undesirable stimulus following a behaviour, decreasing the likelihood of that behaviour recurring. For example, receiving criticism or experiencing discomfort as a result of procrastination can serve as positive punishment, discouraging the habit of procrastinating.

Negative Punishment

Taking away something desirable after a bad habit. Skipping chores might mean missing a movie night. Losing the fun activity discourages skipping chores again. Negative punishment involves the removal of a desirable stimulus following a behaviour, also decreasing the likelihood of that behaviour recurring. For instance, losing access to leisure activities or privileges due to poor time management can serve as negative punishment, discouraging the habit of wasting time.

While punishment can be effective in the short term for suppressing undesired behaviours, it's important to use it judiciously and in conjunction with reinforcement to build lasting habits. Over-reliance on punishment can lead to feelings of resentment, rebellion, or learned helplessness, undermining the effectiveness of habit formation in the long run.

How Extinction Can Help You Break Bad Habits

Habits, good or bad, are hardwired in our brains. But what if you could unlearn a bad habit? That's where extinction comes in!

Imagine a dog trained to get treats for barking. If the treats stop coming, the barking eventually fades away. That's extinction in action! It's the weakening and disappearance of behaviour because it's no longer reinforced. Extinction is the gradual weakening and eventual disappearance of a behaviour due to the lack of reinforcement or punishment. When a previously reinforced behaviour no longer results in the desired outcome, it gradually fades away as the associated neural pathways weaken over time.

To leverage extinction in building effective habits, it's essential to identify and eliminate sources of reinforcement for undesired behaviours while simultaneously reinforcing alternative, more desirable behaviours. For example, if you mindlessly snack while watching TV, remove the snacks from the room. By consistently withholding the reward (snacks), the behaviour (snacking) weakens.

While extinction removes the bad, it's even more powerful when paired with positive reinforcement. Identify a desired behaviour and reward yourself for doing it. This creates a positive cycle, making the good habit more attractive. Continuing with the snacking example, replace the snacks with healthy fruit and reward yourself for enjoying it while watching TV. By consistently rewarding the desired behaviours and withholding reinforcement for undesired behaviours, we can expedite the process of extinction, hastening the transition towards more positive and productive habits.

How We Learn Through Our Actions

Behaviour operates on the environment, and the consequences of behaviour determine whether it will be repeated in the future. Accordingly, behaviour that is followed by pleasant consequences is likely to be repeated, and behaviour followed by unpleasant consequences is less likely to be repeated.

Environmental Influences

Our actions don't exist in a vacuum. The environment reacts to what we do, influencing whether we're more or less likely to repeat those actions in the future. Different responses our actions can evoke are:

Neutral: The Silent Treatment

Imagine spilling your juice at the table. No one yells, but no one cleans it up for you either. This is a neutral operant. The environment offers no reaction, neither encouraging nor discouraging your behaviour of spilling the juice. Neutral responses play a passive role in habit formation. They don't reinforce or punish, so they have little impact on whether you'll be careful with your juice glass next time.

Such as finishing a report on time, but your supervisor is swamped and doesn't acknowledge it or suggesting an idea during a meeting, but it's met with silence from colleagues. It gives a neutral response, and doesn't discourage future idea sharing, but might not encourage it either.

Reinforcers:

The Applause We Crave: Reinforcers are like getting a high five for a job well done. They are environmental responses that make you more likely to repeat a behaviour. There are two main types:

***Positive Reinforcement*:** This is the addition of something pleasant after a behaviour. Such as your superior praises you for exceeding your sales target, which motivates you to work harder next quarter will increase the likelihood of you exceeding future targets. Getting a thumbs up for helping a friend, receiving a raise for good work, or enjoying a delicious snack after finishing your homework are all examples of positive reinforcement.

Negative Reinforcement**:** This might sound negative, but it actually strengthens a behaviour! It involves the removal of something unpleasant after a behaviour. Such as you stay late to finish a project and avoid a potential client's deadline miss, preventing a stressful next day, reinforces staying late to avoid future deadline issues. Taking an umbrella because it's raining to avoid getting wet or putting on headphones to block out noisy neighbours are both examples of negative reinforcement. In both cases, an unpleasant outcome is avoided, making you more likely to repeat the behaviour that led to the avoidance.

Punishers: The Discouraging Response

Punishers are the opposite of reinforcers. They are environmental responses that make you less likely to repeat a behaviour. Just like a frown from your teacher might discourage talking in class, punishers act as deterrents. Here are the two types:

Positive Punishment: This is the addition of something unpleasant after a behaviour. Such as, consistently arriving late for work leads to a formal warning from your manager, making you more likely to be on time in the future is a positive punishment which discourages future tardiness. Getting detention for skipping class, a speeding ticket for exceeding the limit, or a bad grade on a poorly studied test are all examples of positive punishment.

Negative Punishment: This involves the removal of something desirable after a behaviour. Such as, missing a deadline, results in losing out on a project lead opportunity, making you prioritise deadlines more in the future is Negative punishment which discourages missing deadlines. Losing your phone privileges for bad behaviour, having to stay in at recess for misbehaving in class, or missing out on a fun activity because you forgot to do your chores are all examples of negative punishment.

Through consistent awareness, you can gradually transform your procrastination habit and develop more productive work habits. By reinforcing your desired behaviours with rewards, creating a supportive environment, and imposing consequences for procrastination, you create the conditions for success and achievement.

11 MINIMALISM

"Perfection is achieved, not when there is nothing more to add, but when there is nothing left to take away."

– Antoine de Saint-Exupéry,

The term "minimalism" originated in the art world in the 1950s and 1960s, primarily in New York City. Artists such as Donald Judd, Frank Stella, and others began to produce artworks characterised by extreme simplicity and minimal decoration, often consisting of geometric shapes or monochromatic canvases. This movement aimed to strip away any excess and focus on essential elements, challenging traditional notions of art and aesthetics. Over time, the concept of minimalism expanded beyond art to influence various fields, including design, architecture, lifestyle, and even philosophy.

Minimalism extends far deeper into a philosophy that advocates for simplicity, clarity, and intentionality in all aspects of life. Minimalism is about stripping away the non-essential to focus on what truly matters. Minimalism encourages us to eliminate the clutter—not just on our desks, but in our tasks, commitments, and digital spaces. It enhances focus, reduce stress, and elevate efficiency.

Less is more.

-Ludwig Mies van der Rohe

The minimalist approach starts with a critical evaluation of how we allocate our time and energy. It involves asking tough questions about our tasks and commitments: Is this necessary? Does it align with my goals? Does it add value to my life or the lives of others? By applying a minimalist lens, we can identify and eliminate superfluous tasks, delegate responsibilities that do not require our unique skills, and streamline our to-do lists to focus on high-impact activities.

"The more you leave out, the more you highlight what you leave in."

– Henry Green

Minimalism extends to digital, mental and material space. By embracing minimalism in these various aspects, we create space for what truly matters.

Digital Minimalism

In an era where technology permeates every facet of life, the concept of digital minimalism emerges as a must for maintaining focus. Digital Browsing exhausts our mind, leaving little scope for creativity and thinking.

Digital minimalism is a strategy for using technology intentionally and sparingly, ensuring that each digital tool or platform we engage with adds true value to our lives, rather than detracting from it.

Digital minimalism is the idea of intentional use of technology. It's not about rejecting technology altogether but about adopting a more selective approach to digital tools and media consumption. Before integrating any digital tool or platform into your life, have a clear understanding of why you're using it and how it serves your values and objectives. If a tool doesn't support your goals or enhance your life in a meaningful way, it might not merit your attention. For the digital tools that do serve a clear purpose, optimise their use to enhance their value. This might involve customising notifications to reduce distractions, using features that streamline your workflow, or setting specific boundaries around use to prevent overconsumption.

Periodically review your digital tools and media consumption habits. Unsubscribe from unnecessary email lists, uninstall apps that you don't use or that contribute to aimless scrolling and clean up your digital files and folders to maintain a clear digital space.

Be mindful of your media consumption. Choose quality over quantity, select sources that truly inform or enrich you, and avoid falling into the trap of endless browsing, which can consume vast amounts of time and mental energy.

Establish boundaries for tech use. Designate certain areas of your home, such as the bedroom or dining table, as tech-free zones. Similarly, set aside times of the day, perhaps during meals or before bed, where digital devices are put away to encourage more direct engagement with the world and people around you. When using social media or other digital platforms, do so with intention. Engage with content that adds value, contribute meaningfully to discussions, and avoid passive scrolling, which often leads to increased dissatisfaction and decreased productivity.

With fewer digital distractions and a more intentional approach to technology use, you can achieve deeper focus and higher productivity in both your personal and professional life. Reducing digital clutter and mindless consumption will decrease feelings of overwhelm, anxiety, and comparison, contributing to a greater sense of well-being.

By adopting a minimalist approach to our digital lives, we can focus our time, attention, and energy toward activities and connections that truly matter.

In the digital age, the line between connectivity and overstimulation has become increasingly blurred. Digital media like social media, streaming services, news outlets, and more—has become an integral part of our daily lives. While it offers unparalleled access to information and entertainment, its impact on sleep and wellbeing.

Digital media captivates our attention through instant gratification, endless content, and the dopamine-driven feedback loops of social interactions online. The allure of "just one more episode" or "another scroll through the feed" can delay bedtime, cutting into precious sleep hours.

The impact of blue light emitted by screens interferes with the production of melatonin, the hormone responsible for regulating sleep-wake cycles. Exposure to screens before bedtime can disrupt the body's natural circadian rhythm, making it harder to fall asleep and affecting the quality of rest. Leveraging features like "Night Mode" on devices can mitigate some blue light exposure, though it's not a cure-all solution.

Compromised sleep doesn't just lead to next-day grogginess; it has far-reaching effects on cognitive functions, including memory, decision-making, and creativity.

In a counterintuitive twist, sleep deprivation can lead to increased use of digital media, creating a vicious cycle. Tired individuals may rely on the stimulating effects of screen time to counteract fatigue, only to further jeopardise their sleep quality.

To combat the negative impacts of digital media on sleep and productivity, a proactive approach is necessary. Establishing a tech-free window before bedtime will help in winding down and preparing the body for rest call it digital curfews. Being selective about content, especially avoiding stimulating or stress-inducing media before sleep, will promote relaxation. Keeping devices out of the bedroom ensures that the sleep environment is conducive to rest. Developing pre-sleep routines like reading, meditation, or light stretching can replace screen time with more sleep-friendly habits.

Material Minimalism

Simplicity is the ultimate sophistication

-Leonardo da Vinci

A cluttered environment can lead to a cluttered mind, with distractions that impede our ability to concentrate and produce our best work. Minimalism in the physical workspace means having only what you need within arm's reach, creating a serene and orderly environment that promotes concentration. Regularly assess your workspace for items that are not essential to your daily tasks and remove them.

Material minimalism is not merely about decluttering our physical spaces; it's a mindset shift towards prioritising quality over quantity, simplicity over complexity, and experiences over possessions. By embracing material minimalism, we can free ourselves from the burden of excessive consumption, cultivate a deeper appreciation for the things that truly matter, and create space for more meaningful and fulfilling lives.

Material minimalism is living with less and focusing on what is essential. At its core, material minimalism is about intentional living – consciously choosing to simplify our lives by reducing the number of possessions we own and the distractions that clutter our environment. By paring down our belongings to only the things that add value and bring us joy, we can create a sense of clarity, tranquillity, and freedom in our lives.

Material minimalism is not synonymous with deprivation or austerity. Instead, it's about making deliberate choices that align with our values, prioritising experiences, relationships, and personal growth over material possessions. Material minimalism encourages us to question the societal norms and cultural pressures that equate success and happiness with wealth, status, and consumption, and instead, redefine these concepts on our own terms.

By decluttering our physical spaces and simplifying our lives, material minimalism helps us cut through the noise and distractions that often overwhelm us. With fewer possessions vying for our attention, we can focus on what truly matters, set clear priorities, and pursue our goals with greater clarity and purpose.

By letting go of the need to accumulate material wealth and possessions, we can cultivate a sense of contentment and inner peace that transcends external circumstances. Material minimalism encourages us to find fulfilment in experiences, relationships, and personal growth rather than in the accumulation of stuff.

Material minimalism also aligns with principles of environmental sustainability by promoting conscious consumption and reducing our ecological footprint. By consuming less and choosing products that are durable, ethically produced, and environmentally friendly, we can minimise waste, conserve natural resources, and contribute to a more sustainable future for generations to come.

Embrace Material Minimalism by decluttering your physical spaces, one area at a time. Be mindful of the items you own and consider whether each item adds value or serves a purpose in your life. Donate or sell items that no longer bring you joy or serve a practical function, and resist the urge to replace them with unnecessary purchases. Shift your focus from acquiring material possessions to accumulating experiences that enrich your life and create lasting memories. Invest your time and resources in activities that bring you joy, fulfilment, and a sense of connection with others. Avoid impulse buying and consumerism-driven trends, and opt for quality over quantity whenever possible. Foster a mindset of gratitude for the things you already have and the experiences that enrich your life.

Mental Minimalism

Mental minimalism is decluttering our minds, simplifying our thoughts, and cultivating a sense of clarity and peace amidst the chaos of modern life. Minimalist principles and practices will free ourselves from the burden of unnecessary mental baggage and create space for creativity, focus, and inner calm.

Mental minimalism is about prioritising quality over quantity, depth over breadth, and simplicity over complexity in our thinking and mental processes. It involves decluttering our minds from distractions, worries, and unnecessary thoughts, and focusing on what truly matters to us. Just as physical minimalism encourages us to cut down our possessions and live with less, mental minimalism encourages us to simplify our minds and live with greater clarity and intention.

Mental clutter refers to the accumulation of unnecessary thoughts, worries, and distractions that cloud our minds and drain our energy. To embrace mental minimalism, we must learn to let go of these mental burdens and cultivate a sense of inner peace and tranquillity. This involves practising mindfulness meditation, journaling, or engaging in activities that promote relaxation and stress relief.

Mental minimalism encourages us to focus our attention and energy on the essentials – the thoughts, beliefs, and goals that are truly important to us. By prioritising what matters most and letting go of distractions, we can create space for clarity, purpose, and meaningful action in our lives.

Embracing Simplicity

Simplifying our thoughts and mental processes is central to the practice of mental minimalism. This may involve decluttering our minds from excessive rumination, overthinking, and complexity. It requires us to embrace simplicity, clarity, and efficiency in our thinking. By streamlining our mental processes, we can enhance our creative problem-solving abilities.

In today's digital age, we are bombarded with a constant stream of information and stimuli that can overwhelm our minds and lead brain fog. To embrace mental minimalism, consider setting boundaries around your information consumption, such as limiting your time on social media, unsubscribing from unnecessary emails, and curating your news sources to focus on what truly matters to you.

Declutter Your Environment

What you see is what you see.

-Frank Stella

Our physical environment can have a significant impact on our mental clutter. To support mental minimalism, take steps to declutter your physical space and create an environment that promotes calmness and focus. This may involve simplifying your possessions, organising your workspace, and surrounding yourself with objects that bring you joy and inspiration.

Our physical surroundings often mirror the state of our minds. Just as clutter can overwhelm our physical space, it can also clutter our thoughts, hindering clarity, focus, and peace of mind. Take time to declutter and organise your desk, filing cabinets, and digital files. Establish systems and routines to streamline your workflow and minimise distractions. A clutter-free workspace not only fosters efficiency but also cultivates a sense of calm and order that supports mental clarity and well-being.

In addition to decluttering and organising your physical space, surround yourself with objects that bring you joy and inspiration. Display meaningful artwork, photographs, or mementoes that evoke positive emotions and memories. Incorporate elements of nature, such as plants or natural light, to create a serene and uplifting atmosphere. By curating your environment mindfully, you can cultivate a sense of harmony and balance that nourishes your soul.

By simplifying your possessions, organising your workspace, and surrounding yourself with joy and inspiration, you support mental minimalism. Embrace the transformative power of decluttering and discover the profound impact on your mind.

Gratitude

Cultivating an attitude of gratitude is a powerful way to embrace mental minimalism and shift your focus from scarcity to abundance. Take time each day to reflect on the things you are grateful for, whether it's the beauty of nature, the support of loved ones, or the simple pleasures of life. By cultivating gratitude, you can cultivate a mindset of abundance and contentment, reducing brain fog and enhancing your overall well-being.

Embracing mental minimalism is a journey of self-discovery and self-care. By simplifying our thoughts, decluttering our minds, and focusing on what truly matters, we can create space for clarity, creativity, and inner peace in our lives. Whether through mindfulness meditation, limiting information consumption, or practising gratitude, there are many ways to embrace mental minimalism and cultivate a sense of simplicity and serenity in our thoughts and daily lives. By prioritising mental clarity and peace of mind, we unlock our full potential and live with greater purpose, intention.

Three areas of Minimalism

12 RECHARGE – REFUEL – REIMAGINE

Managing stress and understanding the importance of taking breaks is crucial for maintaining mental clarity and preventing burnout.

Sleep

Health is the first muse, and sleep is the condition to produce it.

Ralph Waldo Emerson

Significance of sleep is a fundamental aspect of our existence. There is an intricate relationship between sleep, productivity, and creativity. Sleep is more than just a break from our busy lives; it's a crucial part of our existence that rejuvenates both our minds and spirits.

The benefit of sleep goes beyond just its physical benefits. Sleep is a time when our souls find peace, away from the worries and stresses of daily life. It's like a sanctuary where our minds can rest and recharge, ready to face the world anew when we wake up. Sleep is a time for creativity to flourish. In our dreams our minds roam freely, exploring new ideas and possibilities. It's during these moments of rest that we often find inspiration, paving the way for fresh perspectives and innovative thinking when we're awake.

Sleep serves as a critical mechanism for the restoration and rejuvenation of the body, allowing it to replenish its energy reserves and repair any physical exertions or injuries sustained during waking hours. Sleep is a vital component for a healthy life.

\

Sleep provides a necessary respite for the mind, allowing it to disengage from the sensory stimuli and cognitive demands of waking life. This period of mental rest is essential for preserving cognitive faculties and preventing mental fatigue and exhaustion. Sleep is helpful in sustaining cognitive function and mental clarity.

The role of sleep-in memory consolidation and learning is vital. During sleep, the brain engages in intricate processes of information processing and memory consolidation, enhancing the retention of knowledge and the formation of memories. This cognitive aspect of sleep is crucial for facilitating intellectual growth and the acquisition of new skills. The quality of our sensory experiences during waking hours impacts our ability to enter into a state of restful sleep. An overstimulation of the senses or an excessive preoccupation with sensory input can hinder the transition into sleep, leading to disturbances in sleep patterns and overall sleep quality. Sensory stimuli, such as blue light from digital devices, constant use of moving content on digital media influence our sleep patterns offers.

During sleep our brains consolidate memories, process information, and rejuvenate. Lack of sleep can impair cognitive functions, reduce concentration, and increase irritability, severely impacting productivity. Individual sleep needs vary, most adults require between 7-9 hours of sleep per night for optimal functioning. Ensuring 7-9 hours of quality sleep per night enhances problem-solving skills, creativity, and the ability to focus. Both insufficient and excessive sleep duration negatively impact productivity.

Quality of sleep is just as important as quantity. Poor sleep quality, characterised by frequent awakenings, disruptions, or insufficient time spent in restorative sleep stages such as REM sleep impairs cognitive function. Sleep disorders like insomnia, sleep apnea, stress, noise, light exposure, and uncomfortable sleep environments all contribute to poor sleep quality.

Chronic sleep deprivation or acute sleep loss such as pulling an all-nighter has severe consequences for productivity and safety. Sleep-deprived individuals are more prone to errors, accidents, and lapses in attention, leading to decreased performance. Chronic sleep deprivation is associated with numerous health problems, including obesity, cardiovascular disease, and mental health disorders.

Nourishment

Just as the quality of our sensory input influences our ability to attain restful sleep, so too does our dietary intake play a crucial role in shaping brain function and productivity.

In yoga philosophy, food is considered not only as sustenance for the body but also as a vital source of energy that directly influences our mental, emotional, and spiritual well-being. The quality of the food we consume significantly impacts our productivity, clarity of mind, and overall vitality.

Consumption of sattvic foods such as fresh fruits and vegetables, whole grains, nuts, seeds, and legumes promotes balance, clarity, and tranquillity. These foods are light, easily digestible, and rich in vital nutrients, making them ideal for sustaining energy levels and promoting mental alertness.

Processed foods, fried foods, and foods high in sugar and fat dull the mind and lead to lethargy and inertia. Caffeine, spicy foods, and overly stimulating foods, agitate the mind and contribute to restlessness and anxiety.

Practice of mindful eating in a calm, relaxed environment, free from distractions, and a feeling of gratitude improves digestion and absorption of nutrients. Overeating or consuming heavy, rich foods weighs down the body and mind, leading to sluggishness.

However, mindful eating goes hand-in-hand with another crucial factor: sufficient vitamins and minerals, fuel not only our bodies, but also our minds. A balanced diet rich in essential nutrients keeps us energised, focused, and ready to tackle the day.

Our brain is like a giant orchestra with millions of tiny musicians – brain cells! These brain cells chat with each other using electrical signals and chemicals. This conversation shapes how we think, feel, and act.

To keep this orchestra playing its best music, we need to feed it the right foods. Just like musicians need different instruments, our brain needs different vitamins and minerals for different tasks.

B vitamins (especially B6, B12, and folic acid) are like conductors. They help our brain cells talk clearly to each other, so we can remember things, focus well, and think sharply. Iron, magnesium, and vitamin D are the rhythm section. They keep our brain and body energised throughout the day, helping us avoid fatigue. Omega-3 fatty acids and tryptophan are like mood tuners. They help us stay calm and happy, making it easier to concentrate and get things done. Vitamins C and E are like protectors for our brain cells. They keep them healthy so we can think clearly and learn new things easily.

To keep our brain orchestra in perfect harmony, we should eat a variety of colourful fruits, vegetables, and whole grains. Don't forget to drink plenty of water too! If you are worried about not getting all the nutrients you need, talking to a doctor about supplements might be a good idea.

While multivitamins promise a handy way to plug holes in our diet, there's a fine line between helpful supplementation and the dangers of overdoing it. These supplements often contain a spectrum of essential vitamins and minerals, making them seem like a simple strategy to boost our overall health. They act like an insurance policy against deficiencies, especially for people with picky eating habits, busy schedules, or certain health issues that affect nutrient absorption.

However, the convenience of multivitamins can mask some hidden risks. Fat-soluble vitamins like A, D, E, and K, get stored in our body tissues, and taking too much of them for a long time can lead to a toxic buildup. For example, excessive vitamin A can cause vision trouble, bone pain, and liver damage, while too much vitamin D can harm the kidneys and lead to hypercalcemia i.e. too much calcium in the blood.

Minerals like iron and zinc can also be problematic. High doses can interfere with how our bodies absorb other essential minerals, creating imbalances that show up as fatigue, joint pain, and even neurological issues.

The productivity boosts we're hoping for from multivitamins can quickly turn into a productivity paradox. Too much of a good thing can lead to bad results. Overdoing it on vitamins can cause side effects like nausea, dizziness, and headaches, affecting our focus, memory, and decision-making. The stress on our bodies from these imbalances can also make us feel anxious and irritable, which are not qualities that help us perform well.

So, what can we do?

- Focus on getting your nutrients from a varied and balanced diet. Use multivitamins as a supplement, not a replacement, for whole foods.
- Talk to your doctor about your specific needs. They will assess your diet, lifestyle, and any health

conditions you have to determine if you need a multivitamin and which one is right for you.

- Choose a multivitamin that addresses your specific needs and avoid those with a megadose of vitamins and minerals that could lead to toxicity.

By taking this balanced approach, you can ensure you're giving your body the right fuel to perform at its peak!

Physical Activity

In tandem with mindful eating practices, engaging in regular physical activity further amplifies productivity by boosting mood, energy levels, and mental clarity. Regular physical activity to boost mood, energy levels, and mental clarity. Exercise stimulates the release of endorphins, which reduce stress and promote a sense of well-being, making it easier to tackle daily tasks.

Engaging in regular physical activity helps boost energy levels by improving blood circulation and oxygen flow throughout the body. This increase in energy can lead to heightened alertness and concentration, allowing us to tackle tasks with greater efficiency and focus. Physical activity enhances cognitive function, memory, attention, and problem-solving skills. Regular exercise will sharpen mental acuity, making it easier to process information, make decisions, and generate creative ideas.

Exercise is a powerful stress reliever, helping to lower levels of stress hormones such as cortisol and adrenaline. By providing a natural outlet for tension and anxiety, physical activity promotes relaxation and mental clarity, enabling individuals to approach tasks with a calmer demeanour.

Chronic stress can be one of the biggest enemies of productivity, clouding judgement, and scattering focus. Developing strategies for stress management is essential for maintaining mental health and focus. Yoga, meditation, and deep-breathing techniques significantly reduce stress, improve focus, and enhance cognitive function. Setting realistic deadlines, delegating tasks, and maintaining a clear distinction between work and personal time are also effective strategies for keeping stress at bay.

Regular physical activity improves sleep quality and duration. Adequate rest is essential for cognitive function, mood regulation, and overall well-being. By promoting better sleep pattern and exercise you will feel more refreshed and alert during waking hours.

Taking regular breaks is a proven strategy to boost productivity and creativity. Short breaks during work, "micro breaks," helps maintain consistent performance throughout the day. Longer breaks, such as lunch breaks or weekend activities, provide necessary downtime, allowing the mind to rest and replenish. The concept of a "break" can vary widely, from a walk outside to a hobby or simply doing nothing; what matters is stepping away from work to recharge.

Integrating healthy habits into our daily routines is not just beneficial for our physical well-being but is also a critical component of sustained productivity. By prioritising sleep, nutrition, and exercise, actively managing stress, and recognising the value of breaks, we enhance our focus, creativity, and performance. Health and productivity are inextricably linked, and nurturing one invariably supports the other.

Breathing

One of the most fundamental yet often overlooked aspects of enhancing productivity in life is the very essence of life itself: breathing. There is a profound connection between breathing and productivity. Mindful breathing practices can significantly enhance focus, reduce stress, and elevate overall work performance.

Breathing, at its core, is an automatic and essential function of the body, crucial for delivering oxygen to our cells and removing carbon dioxide, a by-product of metabolism. This process is fundamental to our survival, but its impact extends far beyond mere sustenance. The manner in which we breathe, its depth, rhythm, and rate, plays a significant role in influencing the autonomic nervous system (ANS), which is pivotal in managing various involuntary bodily functions, including heart rate, digestion, respiratory rate, pupillary response, urination and sexual life.

The ANS is composed of two main branches, the sympathetic nervous system (SNS) and the parasympathetic nervous system (PNS). These two branches work in tandem to maintain homeostasis, or balance, within the body.

Breathing serves as a powerful tool to regulate our physiological and psychological state by directly impacting the balance between the sympathetic nervous system (SNS) and the parasympathetic nervous system (PNS). The nature of our breathing—whether it's rapid and shallow or slow and deep can trigger these systems, leading to significant changes in our body's state of arousal or relaxation.

The sympathetic nervous system (SNS) is often referred to as the "fight or flight" system. It becomes activated in response to stress or perceived threats, preparing the body for action. When the SNS is engaged, physiological changes occur to help the body respond to the perceived danger. These changes include an increase in heart rate, dilation of the pupils, redirection of blood flow to vital organs, and heightened alertness. Rapid and shallow breathing, characteristic of the SNS response, helps oxygenate the blood and supply energy to the muscles, facilitating a rapid response to the perceived threat. When faced with a perceived threat or high-stress situation, the SNS kicks into gear, preparing the body to either confront the challenge or escape from it. This activation leads to a series of physiological responses: the heart rate increases, muscles tense up, and the body becomes primed for action. While this response is crucial for survival in dangerous situations, chronic activation due to stress can lead to a continual state of tension and arousal, which can be detrimental to health and well-being.

On the other hand, the parasympathetic nervous system (PNS) is often called the "rest and digest" system. It promotes relaxation and restoration by conserving energy and facilitating bodily functions during times of rest. When the PNS is active, heart rate and breathing slow down, digestion is stimulated, and muscles relax. Deep and slow breathing, associated with the PNS response, helps induce a state of calmness and relaxation, allowing the body to recover and recharge.

Slow, deep, and mindful breathing, often involving diaphragmatic breathing where the abdomen expands with each inhale and contracts with each exhale, has a profoundly different effect on the body. This type of breathing encourages full oxygen exchange and is more efficient than shallow chest breathing. More importantly, it serves as a signal to activate the PNS, which is responsible for the "rest and digest" functions of the body.

The balance between the SNS and PNS is crucial for overall well-being and productivity. In times of acute stress or danger, the activation of the SNS is necessary for survival. However, chronic activation of the SNS due to ongoing stress can lead to health problems and hinder productivity in the long run. Therefore, cultivating mindful breathing practices that promote activation of the PNS, such as slow and deep breathing, can help counteract the detrimental effects of chronic stress, enhance relaxation, and improve focus and productivity in the workplace.

One of the key mechanisms through which deep breathing induces relaxation is the stimulation of the vagus nerve. The vagus nerve is one of the longest nerves in the body and a critical component of the PNS. It extends from the brainstem down through the neck, thorax, and into the abdomen, innervating various organs along the way. When deep breathing activates the vagus nerve, it sends a message to the brain to initiate a relaxation response: the heart rate slows, blood pressure decreases, and muscle tension eases. This shift towards a parasympathetic state supports a calming and restorative process in the body, countering the effects of stress and arousal.

The stimulation of the vagus nerve through deep breathing not only relaxes the body but also has a positive impact on mental health. It can reduce anxiety, lower stress levels, and improve mood, which are essential for maintaining focus and productivity. By consciously applying deep breathing techniques, individuals can effectively manage their stress response, fostering a state of calmness and relaxation even in the face of potential stressors.

By consciously applying proper breathing techniques, such as diaphragmatic breathing and deep breathing using the diaphragm, one can enhance the body's parasympathetic response. This shift not only counteracts the physical symptoms of stress but also fosters a mental state that is more conducive to focus and productivity. When the body is relaxed and the mind is calm, cognitive functions such as problem-solving, memory, and concentration are significantly improved.

Several breathing techniques have been identified as particularly beneficial for improving concentration and productivity. Practices such as diaphragmatic breathing, 4-7-8 breathing, and alternate nostril breathing not only increase oxygen flow to the brain but also promote a state of mental clarity and relaxation, enabling individuals to tackle tasks with enhanced efficiency and creativity.

4-7-8 Breathing, developed by Dr. Andrew Weil, involves inhaling for 4 seconds, holding the breath for 7 seconds, and exhaling for 8 seconds. This pattern can help reduce anxiety and improve concentration.

Pranayama

The ancient practice of pranayama, a fundamental aspect of yoga, also focuses on controlling the breath to optimise physical, mental, and emotional well-being. Pranayama derives from the Sanskrit words "prana," meaning life force or vital energy, and "ayama," meaning extension or expansion. Thus, pranayama can be understood as the extension and regulation of vital energy through breath control. Breathing is an autonomic function, yet it's also under conscious control. Harnessing this control can influence physical and mental states.

Ashtanga Yoga, an ancient system of spiritual practice outlined in the Yoga Sutras of Patanjali, offers profound insights into the connection between breath, life, and consciousness. At the heart of Ashtanga Yoga lies the concept of Pranayama, the regulation and control of breath, which serves as a gateway to higher states of awareness and self-realisation.

अथ योगानुशासनम्॥

योगश्चित्तवृत्तिनिरोधः॥

Now, the teachings of yoga.

Yoga is the cessation of the fluctuations of the mind.

In these profound verses from the Yoga Sutras, Patanjali sets the stage for the practice of yoga, which is ultimately aimed at quieting the restless movements of the mind with pranayama occupying a central place among its practices. Pranayama involves conscious control and regulation of the breath, with the aim of harmonising the flow of prana, or life force energy, within the body. Through various breathing techniques, the practitioner learns to expand and refine their breath, thereby influencing the subtle energy channels (nadis) and centres (chakras) within the energetic body.

श्वासप्रश्वासयोर्गतिविच्छेदः प्राणायामः॥

Pranayama is the regulation of the incoming and outgoing breaths.

By controlling the breath and the conscious regulation of inhalation (Shvasa) and exhalation (Prashvasa), the practitioner gains mastery over the vital life force, leading to profound effects on physical, mental, and spiritual well-being.

उदानजयाविजयाभ्यां प्राणं प्रतिष्ठाप्या॥

By the conquest of the upward and downward breaths, Prana is firmly established.

Through the mastery of inhalation (Udana) and exhalation (Apana), the vital life force (Prana) becomes firmly established within the practitioner, leading to increased vitality, clarity of mind, and spiritual awakening.

The type of pranayama used within Ashtanga yoga practice is called ujjayi translates to victorious breath. 'The ujjayi breath has an equal length inhale and exhale. It is performed by breathing in and out through the nose, and slightly constricting the glottis at the back of the throat.

One other technique is Deep Abdominal Breathing or Diaphragmatic Breathing. Start by sitting or lying down in a comfortable position. Place one hand on your abdomen and the other on your chest. Inhale deeply through your nose, feeling your abdomen rise as you fill your lungs with air. Exhale slowly through your mouth, feeling your abdomen fall. Repeat this process for several minutes. Deep abdominal breathing increases oxygen supply to the brain, promoting mental clarity and alertness.

Alternate Nostril Breathing is a common practice in yoga, this involves closing one nostril while inhaling through the other, then reversing the process. This technique, known as Nadi Shodhana balances the left and right hemispheres of the brain, enhancing mental clarity and focus.

Incorporating mindful breathing into one's daily routine does not require significant time investment or disruption of work. Simple practices can be integrated into existing workflows, such as taking short breathing breaks, beginning the workday with a brief breathing exercise, or using breathing techniques as a tool for transitioning between tasks. Such practices not only enhance immediate focus and productivity but also contribute to long-term well-being and stress resilience.

Empirical evidence and case studies emphasise the effectiveness of breathing techniques in enhancing productivity. Research has shown that individuals who practice regular mindful breathing report higher levels of focus, lower stress levels, and improved overall work performance. Companies that have introduced mindfulness and breathing programs have observed not only enhanced employee productivity but also increased job satisfaction and decreased absenteeism due to stress-related illnesses.

While breathing may seem like a simple, automatic function, its influence on our physiological and psychological state is profound. Through mindful breathing practices, we can harness this influence to transition our bodies into a more relaxed state, which in turn can enhance our ability to concentrate, remain calm, and be more productive in our daily tasks and challenges.

PART 4 EVERYDAY PRODUCTIVITY

13 ENERGY SCHEDULING

Energy Alignment Scheduling transcends the conventional focus on the clock, urging us to instead synchronise our tasks with our intrinsic energy cycles. Our cognitive abilities, focus, and motivation fluctuate throughout the day in patterns based on our chronotype. Tailoring our schedule enhances our productivity and the quality of our work. As no two individuals' energy cycles are identical. It might involve some trial and error to find the perfect alignment between your tasks and energy levels. Moreover, life's unpredictability necessitates a flexible approach, allowing for adjustments as needed while still striving to match high-priority tasks with high-energy windows.

The first step in Energy Alignment Scheduling is to identify your chronotype, which is essentially your body's natural inclination toward periods of peak alertness and energy. While "morning larks" find themselves most energised in the early hours, "night owls" experience their productive surge later in the day. Observing and recording your energy levels over a period will help pinpoint your peak phases.

Once you've identified your high-energy phases, the next step is to align your most challenging and attention-demanding tasks with these periods. Complex problem-solving, creative endeavours, and strategic planning are ideally suited for these energy peaks. Conversely, routine or less cognitively demanding tasks, such as administrative duties or replying to emails, can be scheduled during your off-peak times when your energy naturally wanes.

Energy Alignment Scheduling also emphasises the importance of breaks and downtime. Rest is not a detour from productivity but a vital component of it. Strategic breaks, especially during low-energy periods, will help recharge your cognitive batteries and prevent burnout. Mindfulness, short walks, or even power naps are incredibly restorative.

Adopting Energy Alignment Scheduling can lead to profound long-term benefits, increased job satisfaction, reduced stress, and a healthier work-life balance. By working with your body's natural rhythms rather than against them, you can unlock a more sustainable and enjoyable path to productivity.

Energy Alignment Scheduling invites us to rethink our approach to time management. It's not merely about finding more hours in the day but about making the hours we have work in harmony with our natural tendencies. This alignment between task and temperament will transform your daily routines, making productivity feel less like a struggle and more like a natural expression of our best selves.

Task Fusion

Task Fusion goal is to intelligently combine activities in a manner that amplifies efficiency without diluting the quality or focus required for each task. This acknowledges the finite nature of time and seeks to optimise it by identifying complementary tasks that can coexist harmoniously, thus enabling us to accomplish more within the same time frame.

The essence of Task Fusion lies in the strategic pairing of tasks that naturally align with each other, allowing for a seamless integration of activities. This requires a keen understanding of the nature of the tasks at hand and their demands on our cognitive and physical resources. Pair a task requiring active engagement with one that is more passive or habitual. For instance, pairing a physical activity like walking or jogging with an intellectual one such as listening to an educational podcast or language learning audio allows both tasks to be completed effectively without one undermining the other.

To implement Task Fusion effectively, start by listing daily tasks and activities, categorising them based on their nature—cognitive, physical, passive, or active. Look for opportunities where a passive task can be coupled with an active one without competing for the same type of attention or energy. For example, mundane household chores like cleaning or cooking can be excellent opportunities to fuse with listening to audiobooks or music making these tasks more engaging and educational.

Task Fusion opens up new avenues for personal and professional growth. By integrating learning opportunities into routine activities, we can accumulate knowledge and skills almost effortlessly over time. This continuous learning can lead to significant personal development and professional advancement, turning otherwise unproductive time into valuable growth opportunities.

While Task Fusion offers numerous benefits, it's crucial to approach it mindfully to avoid cognitive overload or burnout. Ensure that the combined tasks do not overtax your mental or physical capacities and that they genuinely complement each other. It's also important to preserve periods of single-tasking, especially for activities that require deep focus or creativity, to maintain a healthy balance.

The risk with multitasking is it dilutes focus. However, in an era where the pressure to multitask is overwhelming, if we choose to engage in it, it should be done mindfully. This mindful approach ensures we can still concentrate on the tasks that truly matter. Some examples are:

Commuting with Learning: Use your daily commute to listen to industry-related podcasts, language lessons, or audiobooks, transforming travel time into a mobile classroom.

Exercise with Education: Pair your workout sessions with educational or motivational content to stimulate both your body and mind.

Networking Walks: Combine physical activity with professional networking by conducting walking meetings, fostering both health and business relationships.

Task Fusion is more than just a time management tactic; it's a lifestyle approach that encourages us to look at our daily routines through a lens of synergy and efficiency. By thoughtfully pairing tasks, we unlock new levels of productivity and personal development.

Time-Wasters

Our days are filled with a finite number of hours, and minimising time wasters is crucial to unlocking our full potential. In our fast-paced world. Yet, so much of our time gets frittered away on hidden time wasters. Social media notifications that pull us away from important tasks, overflowing inboxes that demand constant attention, and even seemingly harmless activities like multitasking can all be productivity assassins. These time wasters chip away at our focus and leave us feeling overwhelmed and behind schedule.

Limit Social Media and Web Browsing

Social media and aimless web browsing eat into your productive time. Set specific times for these activities or use apps that limit your usage during work hours. Being conscious of the time spent on these activities will help redirect your focus to more productive tasks. Social media and web browsing have become ubiquitous parts of our daily lives. While these technologies offer countless opportunities for connection, entertainment, and information, they are also significant sources of distraction, consuming valuable time and attention that could be better spent on more meaningful pursuits.

Excessive social media and web browsing have a profound impact on our mental health and overall well-being. Endless scrolling through social media feeds, mindless web surfing, and compulsive checking of notifications disrupt our focus, drain our energy, and contribute to feelings of overwhelm and anxiety. Studies have shown that excessive use of social media and web browsing leads to decreased productivity, increased procrastination, and heightened levels of stress and dissatisfaction.

The constant barrage of information and stimuli on social media and the internet lead to cognitive overload and reduced cognitive functioning. The brain's natural ability to concentrate and process information becomes compromised, making it difficult to sustain attention, retain information, and engage in deep, focused work. As a result, our ability to think critically, solve problems, and make decisions suffer, hindering our productivity and effectiveness in both professional and personal spheres.

Establish clear boundaries around your social media and web browsing habits. Determine specific times of day when you'll allow yourself to engage with these platforms and stick to them. For example, designate 30 minutes in the morning, afternoon or evening for checking social media and browsing the web, and avoid using these platforms outside of these designated times. There are various apps and browser extensions available that allow you to block or restrict access to specific websites and apps during certain times of day. Experiment with different tools to find what works best for you and your habits. Find alternative activities to fill the time you would typically spend on social media or web browsing. Rediscover hobbies, spend time outdoors, or connect with friends and family in person.

Engaging in offline activities not only helps reduce screen time but also promotes overall well-being and fulfilment.

Email Management

Email has become an indispensable tool for communication, collaboration, and information exchange. However, the sheer volume of emails we receive on a daily basis can quickly become overwhelming, leading to a sense of frustration, inefficiency, and lost productivity. It is difficult to keep up with important messages and prioritise tasks effectively. In addition to emails, we often receive newsletters, promotional offers, and other non-essential communications, cluttering our inboxes and distracting us from more pressing matters.

The constant stream of incoming emails can create a sense of anxiety and overwhelm, making it challenging to focus on important tasks and maintain a healthy work-life balance. Take advantage of email filters and rules to automatically sort incoming messages into folders based on sender, subject, or keywords. This helps streamline your inbox and ensures that important messages are prioritised.

Eliminate Unnecessary Meetings

Evaluate the necessity of each meeting. Can the objectives be achieved through an email or a quick phone call? If a meeting is essential, keep it concise and to the point, with a clear agenda.

Identify your time wasters and eliminate them. It is ongoing and mindful activity, worth its time and efforts.

Time Blocking

Time is one of our most valuable resources. Yet, we struggle to make the most of it, often feeling overwhelmed by competing demands and endless distractions. At its core, time blocking is about allocating specific periods of time to focus on particular tasks, projects, or activities. Rather than bouncing from one task to another throughout the day, time blocking encourages you to segment your schedule into distinct blocks of time, each dedicated to a specific purpose. By organising your day in this way, you create a structure that fosters focus, minimises distractions, and maximises productivity.

Time blocking offers a range of benefits that can transform your approach to productivity and time management. It helps you prioritise your tasks and allocate your time more effectively. By assigning dedicated blocks of time to important tasks or projects, you ensure that they receive the attention they deserve, rather than getting sidelined by less critical activities.

Time blocking promotes deep work and concentration by minimising context switching and interruptions. By committing to a specific task for a set period of time, you create a focused environment that enables you to immerse yourself fully in the task at hand, leading to greater efficiency and higher-quality output.

Time blocking enhances accountability and self-discipline. When you allocate specific time slots to your tasks and activities, you create a sense of commitment to follow through on your plans. This accountability encourages you to stay on track and resist the temptation to procrastinate or deviate from your schedule.

Time blocking fosters work-life balance by allowing you to allocate time for both work-related tasks and personal activities. By scheduling dedicated blocks of time for relaxation, exercise, or spending time with loved ones, you ensure that your life is not solely dominated by work, leading to greater overall satisfaction and well-being.

To implement time blocking effectively, start by identifying your priorities and goals for the day, week, or month. What tasks or projects do you need to focus on? What deadlines do you need to meet? By clarifying your objectives, you can allocate your time more strategically. Break down your tasks and projects into smaller, more manageable chunks. This will make it easier to allocate specific time blocks to each task and ensure that you make progress toward your goals consistently. Schedule your time blocks according to your natural rhythms and energy levels. Allocate your most challenging or important tasks to times when you're most alert and focused, and save less demanding tasks for times when your energy is lower. Be realistic about your time estimates and leave buffer periods between time blocks to account for unexpected delays or interruptions. This will help you maintain flexibility in your schedule and prevent you from feeling overwhelmed if things don't go according to plan. Some people prefer to block out their entire day in advance, while others prefer to plan their time blocks on a more ad hoc basis. Find what suits your preferences.

Imagine your to-do list overflowing with work emails, data analysis reports, and client calls. Time blocking would be like scheduling separate blocks for each task type throughout your day. While effective for staying organised, it can lead to context switching fatigue. Here's where time batching shines.

Time batching is like tackling similar tasks in themed sprints. You could dedicate a focused morning block to processing all your emails, allowing you to stay in a responsive state of mind and avoid the constant ping-pong of checking your inbox throughout the day. Then, in the afternoon, you might schedule a "data analysis power hour" to churn through those reports while your analytical thinking is sharp. Finally, group all your client calls together to minimise context switching and keep the conversation flow going. By strategically combining time blocking and time batching, you can create a work schedule that offers both structure and flexibility, maximising your productivity and minimising wasted time.

Task Batching

The technique involves grouping similar tasks together and completing them in dedicated blocks of time. By consolidating similar activities into focused sessions, task batching can help maximise efficiency, minimise distractions, and enhance concentration, ultimately leading to greater productivity and improved outcomes. Time blocking focuses on scheduling specific blocks of time for task, time batching involves grouping similar tasks together to increase productivity and efficiency.

Task batching, also known as batch processing or time blocking involves grouping similar tasks together and completing them in dedicated blocks of time. Rather than switching between unrelated tasks throughout the day, task batching allows you to focus on one type of activity at a time, maximising efficiency and minimising cognitive load.

The key principle behind task batching is the concept of context switching cost, which refers to the mental effort and time required to transition between different tasks or types of work. Every time we switch our focus from one task to another, our brains must adjust to the new context, leading to a loss of productivity and increased mental fatigue. By batching similar tasks together, we reduce the frequency of context switches, allowing us to maintain focus and momentum throughout our workday.

While it's important to be ambitious, setting unrealistic deadlines can lead to unnecessary stress and burnout. Estimate the time you need for tasks realistically, considering potential interruptions and breaks.

Effective time management is not about squeezing more tasks into your day but about ensuring that you're spending your time on tasks that align with your goals and values. By implementing these techniques and strategies, you can create a more structured, focused, and ultimately productive daily routine.

14 TEN MINUTES MORNING RITUAL

Our life always expresses the result of our dominant thoughts. It seems essential, in relationship and all tasks, that we concentrate only on what is most significant and important.

Soren Kierkegaard

With the constant barrage of tasks, distractions, and responsibilities, it's easy to feel overwhelmed and lose sight of our goals. This is where the morning planning ritual comes in as a simple yet powerful practice that can transform your productivity and set the tone for a successful day ahead.

The morning planning ritual is more than just creating a to-do list; it's about intentionally setting aside time each morning to reflect, prioritise, and strategies for the day ahead. It's a proactive approach to managing your time and energy, rather than reacting to whatever comes your way.

By taking time in the morning to plan your day, you gain clarity on what needs to be accomplished and can focus your efforts on the most important tasks. With a clear plan in place, you can work more efficiently and effectively, avoiding the trap of busy work and distractions. Knowing what lies ahead and having a plan to tackle it can significantly reduce stress and anxiety, allowing you to approach your day with confidence and calmness. By prioritising tasks and allocating your time wisely, you can make better decisions throughout the day, ensuring that you're focusing on what truly matters.

The morning planning ritual is a small investment of time that yields significant returns in terms of productivity, focus, and overall well-being. By incorporating this simple practice into your daily routine, you can take control of your day and unlock your full potential.

Why 10 minutes?

Dedicating just ten minutes each morning to plan the day can be a transformative practice, turning potential chaos into structured success. It is a simple morning planning ritual yet has a profound impact on personal and professional productivity, offering insights into how this brief investment of time can yield substantial returns throughout the day.

The essence of the ten-minute morning ritual lies in its simplicity and focus. It involves taking a brief pause before the day's activities begin to review, prioritise, and strategies.

Starting the day with a clear understanding of our purpose and aligning our tasks with our core values sets a foundation for meaningful and productive actions. By prioritising tasks that resonate with our personal and professional goals during morning planning, we create a roadmap that not only guides our daily activities but also contributes to our long-term fulfilment and success.

Finding purpose acts as a compass for our lives, guiding our decisions, shaping our goals, and giving context to our actions. It transforms routine tasks into steps towards a larger goal, infusing daily life with significance and direction. Purpose provides resilience in the face of adversity, as it offers a reason to persevere when challenges arise. It enriches our lives, fostering a sense of fulfilment and satisfaction that goes beyond transient pleasures or achievements. Discovering and embracing a purpose elevates our existence from mere survival to a meaningful journey, marked by growth, contribution, and a deeper connection to the world around us.

"Life is never made unbearable by circumstances, but only by lack of meaning and purpose."

-Viktor E. Frankl

Viktor Emil Frankl, born in Vienna in 1905, had a life and work shaped by the tumultuous events of his time, most notably his survival through four Nazi concentration camps during the Holocaust.

Frankl's interest in psychology began at an early age, influenced by the works of Freud and Adler. However, Frankl's perspective on human psychology would take a distinct path, emphasising the search for life's meaning as the central human motivational force. This view was in part shaped by his experiences of suffering, loss, and resilience during the Holocaust.

In the shadow of his harrowing experiences in concentration camps, Frankl developed logotherapy, which posits that the primary drive-in human beings is not pleasure or power, but the pursuit of "meaning." Life has meaning under all circumstances, even the most miserable ones. This belief was not theoretical for Frankl; it was a lived reality during his time in the concentration camps, where finding a sense of purpose was often the difference between life and death.

Those who could find meaning in their suffering were far more resilient to the despair of camp life. We cannot avoid suffering, but we can choose how to cope with it, find meaning in it, and move forward with renewed purpose. By aligning our actions with our deeper values and seeking meaning in even the smallest tasks, we could live more fulfilling lives.

Having a purpose narrow down life's distraction, allowing us to concentrate on what truly matters. This clarity can lead to more effective decision-making and a more focused approach to life's tasks.

Sharpens Focus contributes to enhanced productivity by streamlining one's attention and resources toward high-priority tasks and goals. When we have a clear purpose, they are less likely to be swayed by irrelevant distractions or to engage in activities that don't align with their core objectives. A focused approach ensures that energy and time are invested in tasks that are not only meaningful but also instrumental in achieving desired outcomes. Consequently, decision-making becomes more strategic, and efforts are more targeted, leading to higher efficiency and productivity.

A strong sense of purpose not only clarifies what is important but also amplifies the effectiveness of actions taken toward those ends, thereby boosting overall productivity. Aligning with your purpose in life sets a solid foundation for daily planning. When you understand your overarching goals and what truly matters to you, it becomes much easier to prioritise your daily tasks. This alignment ensures that the activities you plan for each day are not just random or reactionary, but are steps towards fulfilling your larger life objectives.

Planning our day with your purpose in mind transforms routine tasks into meaningful actions, making each day a strategic move towards realising your long-term vision. This intentional approach to daily planning not only enhances productivity but also imbues everyday life with a sense of fulfilment and direction.

Effective daily planning is an art that combines strategic foresight with personal reflection, acting as a catalyst for both personal and professional growth. At its core, this process revolves around three fundamental pillars: Prioritisation, time allocation, and reflection. These components work in harmony to transform ordinary days into meticulously crafted sequences of purpose-driven actions, leading to a more fulfilling and productive life.

The Triad

Effective daily planning is more than just a list of tasks; it's a strategic approach that involves three critical components: Prioritisation, time allocation, and reflection. Mastering these elements can transform your daily planning from a mere to-do list into a powerful tool for personal and professional growth.

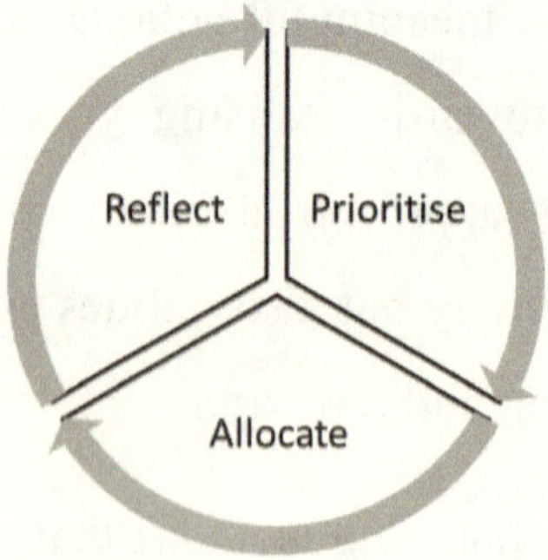

The Triad of Effective Daily Planning

Prioritisation is the Art of Identifying What Truly Matters. Prioritisation is also the Art of Ranking Your Tasks. The ability to prioritise is at the heart of effective planning. Prioritisation starts with a clear understanding of your goals and values, allowing you to identify tasks that align with your long-term objectives. By focusing on what truly matters, you can ensure that your efforts are concentrated on high-impact activities, reducing time wasted on trivial pursuits.

Time Allocation is strategically investing your hours, assigning specific time blocks to tasks based on their priority and the energy they require. Time allocation is not just about squeezing in as many tasks as possible; it's about assigning tasks to the times of day when you're most productive and ensuring there's a balance between work and rest. This mindful approach to scheduling helps in managing your energy levels, preventing burnout, and increasing the quality of your output.

Reflection is the key to continuous improvement. The often overlooked but equally critical component of daily planning is reflection. At the end of each day, taking time to reflect on what was accomplished, what challenges were encountered, and what lessons were learned is vital. Reflection allows you to assess the effectiveness of your prioritisation and time allocation strategies, providing insights that can inform future planning. It's an opportunity to celebrate successes, however small, and to recalibrate your approach based on the day's experiences. Reflection fosters a growth mindset, encouraging continuous improvement and adaptation.

To integrate these three components into your daily life, consider starting your day with a planning session where you prioritise tasks and allocate time to them. his triad not only helps in managing daily tasks more effectively but also in aligning your daily actions with your broader life goals, ensuring that each day is a step towards fulfilling your purpose.

Benjamin Franklin, one of the founding fathers of the United States, a prominent statesman, scientist, and inventor was a man deeply interested in personal improvement and productivity. His approach to planning and time management is famously documented in his autobiography, providing a glimpse into the disciplined routine that underpinned his remarkable achievements.

Franklin's daily schedule explains the importance of structure and intentionality in his day. He carefully divided his day into segments dedicated to work, study, leisure, and reflection, ensuring a balanced approach to his diverse interests and responsibilities.

Franklin's day began early, around 5:00 AM, with a period he termed "The Morning Question," where he asked himself, "What good shall I do this day?" This reflective question set the tone for a day cantered around purpose and productivity. Following this, he allocated time for personal hygiene, breakfast, and planning or preparation for the day's work.

Perhaps one of the most impactful aspects of Franklin's daily routine was his evening reflection. He ended his day with the question, "What good have I done today?" This allowed him to assess his accomplishments, reflect on his actions, and consider areas for improvement. This practice of self-reflection was integral to his philosophy of continuous personal development.

Incorporating this ten-minute planning ritual into the morning routine can have a profound impact on productivity. Beginning the day with a clear plan helps to direct attention to what truly matters, reducing the likelihood of becoming sidetracked by less important tasks. By allocating time to tasks based on their priority, individuals can work more efficiently, ensuring that critical tasks are addressed when energy levels are highest. Having a plan in place alleviates the anxiety of the unknown, providing a sense of control and calmness that enhances overall well-being. A morning review allows for adjustments based on new information, making it easier to adapt to unforeseen changes with minimal disruption.

There are psychological and neurological benefits of morning planning. Morning rituals enhance decision-making, improve time management, and increase cognitive function. The practice of planning engages the prefrontal cortex, responsible for executive functions like focusing attention, predicting outcomes, and controlling impulses, setting a productive tone for the day.

Adopting a new habit requires intention and consistency. Making planning a non-negotiable part of the morning routine, much like brushing your teeth. Choosing a quiet space free from interruptions to ensure the planning session is focused and effective.

The act of writing in a physical planner might seem quaint or outdated. However, this traditional method of planning and organising tasks holds a unique set of benefits that can enhance productivity, clarity, and overall well-being. Writing by hand engages the brain in a more comprehensive way than typing. The act of physically forming letters and words involves a complex set of motor skills and tactile feedback, which in turn, stimulates brain regions associated with learning and memory. When you write down your tasks, goals, and appointments in a planner, the information is more likely to be encoded in your long-term memory, making it easier to recall your plans and commitments.

The process of writing in a physical planner demands a level of engagement and mindfulness that is often absent in digital interactions. The tactile experience of pen on paper, the act of turning pages, and even the opportunity to personalise with handwriting, sketches, or stickers, all contribute to a more immersive planning experience. This mindfulness lead to more thoughtful reflection on priorities, goals, and how time is allocated, fostering a deeper connection to personal and professional objectives.

One of the most significant benefits of a physical planner is the absence of digital distractions. Unlike planning apps and software, a physical planner doesn't come with notifications, pop-up messages, or the temptation to switch tasks to check emails or social media. This isolation from digital interruptions allows for a more focused and uninterrupted planning session, enhancing productivity and the quality of time management.

Physical planners offer a tangible sense of progress that digital tools can sometimes lack. The act of crossing off completed tasks, highlighting important notes, or flipping back through pages to review past achievements provides visual and tactile satisfaction. This physical evidence of progress can be incredibly motivating, reinforcing a sense of accomplishment and encouraging continued productivity.

The act of writing in a planner can also serve as a stress-relieving activity, much like journaling. The methodical process of noting down tasks, appointments, and goals helps to declutter the mind, reducing the anxiety associated with trying to remember numerous commitments. Furthermore, the personalisation of a physical planner can make the planning process a creative outlet, contributing to overall mental well-being.

CONCLUSION

KEYS TO PRODUCTIVITY

As we conclude our journey through the realms of productivity, it's essential to reflect on the key insights gleaned from each maximising chapter and to consider the steps forward. Embracing productivity is not merely about optimising time or output; it's about cultivating a lifestyle that balances efficiency with well-being, purpose with leisure, and growth with contentment.

The journey to enhanced productivity is personal and ongoing. Start with small, manageable changes to build momentum. Productivity is not about perfection but progress. Embrace the principles that resonate with you and adapt them to your unique circumstances and goals.

Productivity is more than a set of strategies; it's a mindset that values purpose, efficiency, and balance. It's about making the most of our time so we can live more fully, not just do more. By embracing the principles outlined in this book, you can create a more organised, efficient, and fulfilling life.

As you move forward, remember that productivity is a journey, not a destination. It's about continuous improvement, learning from experiences, and adapting to change. With each step, you'll discover more about yourself and what it means to live a productive life that aligns with your values and aspirations.

It is not a question of starting. The start has been made. It's a question of what's to be done from now on. - B. F. Skinner

---

Thank you and good luck!

www.ingramcontent.com/pod-product-compliance
Lightning Source LLC
Chambersburg PA
CBHW022142160726
48282CB00024B/167
* 9 7 8 9 3 3 4 1 2 9 5 2 6 *